FAITHS
—— FOR A ——
FUTURE
A RESOURCE FOR TEACHING ENVIRONMENTAL THEMES IN RELIGIOUS EDUCATION

Religious and Moral Education Press
A division of SCM-Canterbury Press Ltd
A wholly owned subsidiary of Hymns Ancient & Modern Ltd
St Mary's Works, St Mary's Plain
Norwich, Norfolk NR3 3BH

First published 1998

ISBN 1 85175 163 7

Faiths for a Future is printed on recycled paper and board.

Acknowledgement
The editor and publisher thank the owners or controllers of copyright for permission to use the copyright material reproduced in this book. Every effort has been made to contact copyright owners and the editor and publisher apologize to any whose rights have inadvertently not been acknowledged.

Designed, typeset and illustrated by Topics – The Creative Partnership, Exeter

Printed in Great Britain by Brightsea Press, Exeter for SCM-Canterbury Press Ltd, Norwich

FAITHS
— FOR A —
FUTURE

A RESOURCE FOR TEACHING ENVIRONMENTAL
THEMES IN RELIGIOUS EDUCATION

Edited by

Robert Vint

for the Religious Education and Environment Programme

REEP

RMEP

RELIGIOUS AND MORAL EDUCATION PRESS

Contents

① Introduction

BY ROBERT VINT

Robert Vint graduated in Ecology and Philosophy before teaching Geography. After organizing conferences and lectures on religions and ecology, he helped found REEP in 1994 and is now its Programme Administrator. He is a Committee Member of the World Congress of Faiths and a Fellow of the RSA.

REEP, the Religious Education and Environment Programme, was created in 1994 with the support of a wide range of environmental and Religious Education charities. It is founded on the conviction that concern for nature is essential to religion and that religious awareness has a vital contribution to make to respect for nature. Its professional development sessions for teachers provide a down-to-earth approach to Religious Education, moral and spiritual development, and assemblies.

REEP and Its Work

What Does REEP Do?

REEP has developed a range of tailor-made training events presented by experienced facilitators with expertise in their chosen field. They provide teachers and schools with relevant information and teaching materials and also offer ideas for practical classroom activities within the framework of the National Curriculum, helping pupils to:

- **experience** the world around them,
- **explore** the relevance of traditional religious teachings about the world,
- **reflect** upon these in order to develop and articulate their own beliefs and values concerning the environment and their place within it,
- then find ways to take practical **action** based upon their own beliefs and values.

This handbook offers teachers some of REEP's most popular classroom activities.

Why Is This Work Needed?

Children are intensely aware of their own environment and yet they grow up into a society that seems to be blindly destroying it.

For their moral and spiritual development children need opportunities to explore and develop their own values and beliefs concerning the world around them.

Exploring the traditional beliefs of their own and other societies helps children both to understand and appreciate these beliefs and to cultivate their own. It introduces them to different ways of seeing and valuing the world and helps them to think clearly about how we should treat the planet.

Why Should RE be 'Green'?

REEP's programme is based on the recognition that there are strong educational, environmental and religious reasons for taking a 'green' approach to RE.

Educational Reasons

Religious Education often comes under attack as out of date, boring and irrelevant to children in the modern world. Education needs to relate to children's interests and to the issues they will face when they are adults.

It has long been known that children have an innate interest in the natural world – whether this is a goldfish in an inner-city classroom or a wide stretch of unspoilt coastline to which only a fortunate few have access. Enlightened education builds upon such natural motivation to help children learn.

Rapidly accelerating destruction of the natural world is threatening our quality of life and potentially our very survival. By the time primary children begin work these issues could be our number one priority.

So studying environmental issues will provide interest and life skills, but why do it in RE if you are already doing it in Science and Geography?

Environmental Reasons

Technology will not, in itself, solve the environmental crisis if our demand for more and more consumer goods continues unabated. No amount of ingenuity would save us from environmental suicide if the whole population of the world succeeded in owning two cars and going on a package holiday each year. Such a level of desire for material things is not traditional and indeed has been condemned by most religions and cultures. These traditions all recommend that we change our motives, change our hearts and minds and ask ourselves what are really the most meaningful things in life.

Whilst it is not our job to impose our own views and values on children, we do have a responsibility to help them explore the range of different views and teachings on these issues so that they do not end up blindly accepting the consumerist values communicated to them by adverts and television.

Religious Reasons

Many parents and teachers do practise a religion and believe either that a divine power created the world or that nature has some kind of purpose beyond filling our shopping-baskets. They would like all children to be at least familiar with these beliefs and values.

Planning Schemes of Work in RE

REEP's approach to RE is based upon guidance from Ofsted:

Good learning in religious education occurs when pupils gain an understanding that religion has practical application to everyday life. At best, pupils are helped to recognise that the scope of religious education is wider than knowledge of Christianity and other major religious traditions and that it relates those traditions to a broad experience of life. Those who have no background of religious faith should come to recognise that religious beliefs can give guidance and motivation in ethical considerations and that, to their holders, beliefs have an explanatory power which gives coherence to aspects of life which might otherwise appear fragmentary and disconnected.

The best starting point for the teaching of religious education is often the questions raised for pupils by moral issues in their own lives. Far from reducing religious education to the discussion of social and personal problems, the teaching should make clear the relationship between religious belief and personal and social behaviour. The ten commandments, for example, can be shown to be particular instances of a concern to uphold moral standards which is found within all religions, and public concerns such as attitudes to war and the use of the earth's resources can be derived, and receive support, from religious traditions.

OFSTED HANDBOOK, 1993, PART 4, SECTION 6.12

Unlike other subjects, RE has locally agreed syllabuses. In England and Wales, these are often, but not always, based on the National Model Syllabuses produced by SCAA in 1994. REEP events have been designed to fit these National Model Syllabuses but can be adapted to the specific needs of any local agreed syllabus. The attainment targets given in the National Model Syllabuses are 'Learning *about* religion' and 'Learning *from* religion'. These or similar attainment targets feature in most local agreed syllabuses and are incorporated into REEP's learning cycle (see page 7).

To help schools plan schemes of work that will deliver their local curriculum, objectives are given for the RE activities in this book. It is hoped that the use of environmental issues as a focus for these activities will suggest links with other subjects such as Science or Geography and help teachers to include RE in cross-curricular planning.

Links with Other Areas

Spiritual, Moral, Social and Cultural Development

SMSC is not the sole responsibility of the RE co-ordinator but should be addressed by all teachers in all subjects and throughout the life of the school. We can see all around us the consequence of teaching that spirituality and morals should concern priests but not economists, scientists or businessmen. If we want to escape from a society in which things we value are destroyed in pursuit of profit, teachers will have to bring spiritual and moral development into the Science and Geography classroom. (See Ofsted Handbook, part 4, pages 15–19.)

That being said, RE still provides unique opportunities for addressing issues that are difficult to cover in other subjects. For example, with an issue like pollution, a Science lesson could look at pollution control technology and a Geography lesson at how pollution damages the natural world, but an RE lesson could examine the underlying issues by exploring religious attitudes to the consumerism and wealth that cause the pollution.

SMSC does not relate only to what is taught but also to the values and conduct of pupils. Religious Education can help pupils to reflect upon their own values and could provide opportunities for them to draw up their own environmental code of conduct or to set up practical school projects based on these values. (See Chapter 8, pages 106–107.)

The following statement on the environment is one of four made by the SCAA National Forum for Values in Education and the Community:

Environment: Values
We value the natural world as a source of wonder and inspiration and accept our duty to maintain a sustainable environment for the future.

Environment: Principles

On the basis of these values we should:
– preserve balance and diversity in nature wherever possible
– justify development in terms of a sustainable environment
– repair habitats devastated by human development wherever possible
– understand the place of human beings within the world

STATEMENT ON VALUES, SCAA NATIONAL FORUM FOR VALUES
IN EDUCATION AND THE COMMUNITY, SEPTEMBER 1996

Environmental Education

Environmental Education is a cross-curricular National Curriculum theme, to be addressed in all subjects. Too often it is confined to Geography and Science lessons. The SCAA guidelines for Environmental Education list the following opportunities for teaching about the environment in RE at Key Stages 1 and 2:

Agreed syllabuses for religious education are defined locally. Model syllabuses published by SCAA 'suggest' rather than 'direct' content and structure for teaching religious education; the opportunities set out below are those offered by the model syllabuses.

KEY STAGE 1

Opportunities
- *content, for example:*
  - *listening to stories and poems which describe God as the creator and the idea of the world as a precious gift to humanity*
- *learning experiences, for example:*
  - *talking about their own feelings about the natural world, such as awe, wonder and a sense of mystery*
  - *distinguishing between what is made and what belongs to the natural world*

KEY STAGE 2

Opportunities
- *content, for example:*
  - *learning about Islamic teaching that humans are the best of Allah's creation*
  - *learning about Sikh teaching that God is One, the Creator and Sustainer and that all human beings are equal in the eyes of God*
- *learning experiences, for example:*
  - *considering Christian (and other) beliefs about God as creator*
  - *talking about their attitudes towards the environment*
  - *considering how they can show their respect for the environment*

TEACHING ENVIRONMENTAL MATTERS THROUGH THE NATIONAL CURRICULUM,
PAGES 56–57, SCAA, 1996

Whole-school Development

Voluntary policies such as the following can be valuable parts of a school development plan and provide a focus for developing the buildings, grounds and links with the local community.

Whole-school Environment Policy

This can include environmental guidelines for school purchases (such as use of recycled paper), energy conservation and provision of recycling bins; policies to reduce use of cars by parents and staff; guidelines for inclusion of environmental issues in the curriculum; an environmental code of conduct drawn up by the pupils, and annual 'environmental audits' to assess how green the school is and where improvements could be made. (See Activities Z1 and Z2, pages 106–107.)

Educational activities for involving children in these issues can be found in *Eco School* (Prue Poulton and Gillian Symons, WWF School Design Project, ISBN 0 947613 27 7).

School-grounds Development

School grounds are not just spaces in which to play football but are potential educational resources that can contribute to all aspects of children's education. In relation to RE, schools could create multifaith gardens, peace gardens, contemplative spaces or gardens of Eden. (See Activity Z3, page 107.)

For guidance on drawing up a school-grounds development plan contact Learning through Landscapes (Tel. 01962 846258).

Local Agenda 21

At the United Nations Earth Summit on Environment and Development in 1992, nearly every nation agreed to ask its local authorities to draw up a local agenda of environmental policies in preparation for the twenty-first century. Schools, churches, community groups and all other local organizations are encouraged to take part – not only in helping draft the local authority's policy but also in drawing up their own policy. Your LEA can put you in touch with your local authority's Agenda 21 Officer (who usually works in the Planning Department).

Teaching Down-to-Earth RE

Systemic and Thematic Approaches to RE

Teachers will often see religions defined as **traditional belief systems** in RE handbooks. This comes from the Westhill Model for teaching RE – a method that provides the basis for REEP's approach. We highly recommend the book *How Do I Teach RE?* (G. Read, J. Rudge, R. Howarth and G. Teece) and related Westhill Project materials (available from Westhill RE Centre, Westhill College, Selly Oak, Birmingham B29 6LL).

Traditional These are long-standing belief systems that have influenced many generations.

Belief These traditional systems of thought are based on belief in a coherent view of the world and how we should live in it.

System Traditional beliefs are not a jumble, they hang together and are all derived from a central world-view.

In REEP's interpretation of the Westhill Model it is recommended that religions are made relevant to children by exploring them as they relate to two other areas:

- **major contemporary issues,**
- **children's individual patterns of belief.**

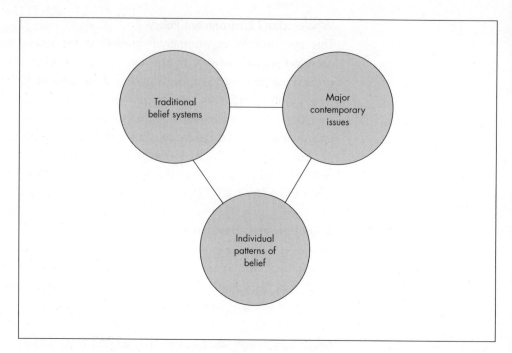

Two different methods are suggested for bringing these areas together: the **systemic** approach and the **thematic** approach.

The **systemic** approach to RE is to explore the whole belief system of one religion as it relates to a range of major contemporary issues. For example, a systemic study of Islam could look at:

• Islamic teachings on khalifah (guardianship) in relation to conservation,
• Islamic teachings on tahwid (oneness) in relation to the order of nature,
• Islamic teachings on zakat (charity) in relation to the planting of trees.

The systemic approach may be represented as follows:

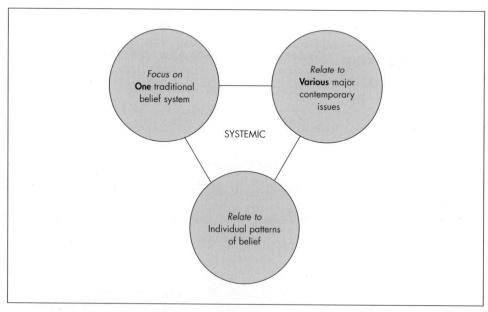

The **thematic** approach to RE is to explore one theme relating to one major contemporary issue in two or more belief systems. For example, a thematic study of 'Caring for the World' could look at how the following teachings relate to the contemporary issue of the destruction of forests:

• Hindu teachings on ahimsa (non-violence),
• Buddhist teachings on interdependence,
• Christian teachings on stewardship.

The thematic approach may be represented as follows:

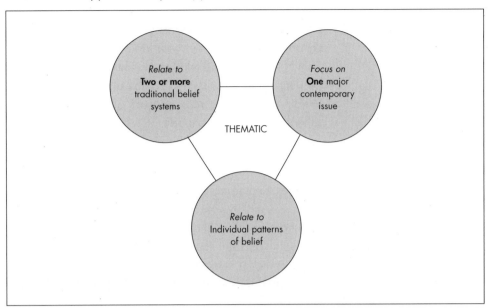

Which Approach Should I Use?

There is a good case for using both methods in order to deliver a rounded curriculum. It is recommended, however, that children have an overview of several individual religions before they start exploring themes across different religions.

REEP's Learning Cycle

Whether you choose a systemic or a thematic approach, we recommend that your lesson plans take the children through a series of learning stages that starts with their own personal experiences and finishes with them expressing their own beliefs and values in a form of practical action.

The four stages used in our training sessions are:

experience ———▶ explore ———▶ reflect ———▶ act

Children should be helped to **experience** the world around them, **explore** the relevance of traditional religious teachings about the world, **reflect** upon these in order to develop their own beliefs and values concerning the environment and their place within it, and then find ways to take practical **action** based upon their own beliefs and values. For example:

(a) Children could initially experience the destruction of nature through the story and illustrations in a book such as *Brother Eagle, Sister Sky* (Susan Jeffers, Hamish Hamilton).

(b) They could next explore religious teachings about stewardship through the story of the Garden of Eden and the Islamic teaching of khalifah (guardianship).

(c) Children could then reflect upon their own beliefs about how people should care for the earth by writing, drawing or painting their own vision of a better future.

(d) Finally one group might suggest acting by supporting an adopt-a-whale scheme.

Let's look at these stages in a little more detail:

Experience Hands-on, direct experience and use of the senses make issues real for children. If, for example, your topic was religious attitudes to trees, could you start by visiting a wood and writing poems about it, or by watching a film on rainforest destruction and discussing it, or by observing and drawing a tree in the playground? What suitable resources (places, objects, stories, people, etc.) are there in your school and neighbourhood?

Activities for experiencing nature are given in Chapter 2 (pages 15–23).

Explore Exploration is about linking together experiences, facts, observations and ideas and making sense of them. For example, if you were exploring Hindu teachings about caring for animals, how do these link to Hindus' views on souls, reincarnation, non-violence, right diet and the belief that some kinds of animal are sacred? How might some of these views be relevant to modern animal welfare issues – from abandoned pets to factory farming? How might the world differ if everyone followed these beliefs?

Reflect Reflection is about relating what is being explored to personal views, beliefs and values. For example, if children are studying religious teachings on wealth, poverty or simple living then how does this affect their own views? Do they want to be the richest person in the world or are their own desires somewhat different?

Activities for exploring and reflecting upon the beliefs of five major world religions are given in Chapters 3–7.

Act People act all the time in ways based on their own beliefs and values. What we buy, how we spend our holidays, how we treat our friends, what we eat and what charities we support are all determined by our beliefs and values. Schools also have some collective beliefs and values and expect staff and pupils to act in certain ways and not others – even if the reasons are never discussed. If we take the development of our beliefs and values and those of pupils seriously then it is important that we all have opportunities to change individually and collectively the ways we act.

Action activities are given in Chapter 8 (pages 106–107).

Exploring and Reflecting upon Religious Beliefs and Values

In our framework we have found it useful to group religious beliefs and values under four subheadings:

- **Teachings about the World**
- **Spiritual Teachings**
- **Moral Teachings**
- **Visions of the Future**

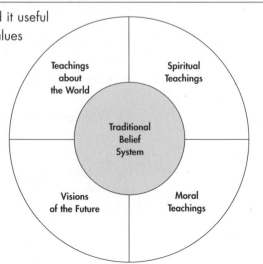

Teachings about the World Traditional belief systems are founded upon a 'cosmology' or set of teachings about where the world came from, what it is like and what our place in it is.

Spiritual Teachings Within the context of cosmological beliefs relating to a particular religion, there exists a set of teachings about how people can experience, relate to and respond to the world and to its creator or origin.

Moral Teachings From these spiritual teachings can be derived teachings about how people should and should not behave towards the rest of the world and towards its creator or origin.

Visions of the Future Finally, in the light of all these teachings, the followers of a religion have visions or ideals about the kind of world we should live in and what we need to do to help that world come about.

For example, we could explore Christianity in this way as follows:

Exploring Some Christian Beliefs and Values

Christian Teachings about the World

- God created the world in a state of harmony.
- God is present everywhere in his world.
- Humans are continually called to help God protect his world.

Christian Spiritual Teachings

This means that:
- Humans can encounter God and his works anywhere in his world.
- Humans can discover what God wants them to do through prayer.

Christian Moral Teachings

Through these spiritual practices Christians realize that they are called by God:

- To share
- Not to kill
- To live simply
- To protect the environment

Christian Visions of the Future

Based upon this:
- Christians look forward to a time when nature will be renewed and harmony restored, when 'The wolf and the lamb shall feed together' (Isaiah 65:25).
- Christians believe they should help restore the world to the state of harmony in which God made it, to build God's kingdom on earth.
- Christians believe this can be done by following the spiritual and moral teachings of their religion.
- This is what Christians are trying to do in their monasteries and other communities.
- St Francis is an example of someone who tried to do this through the way he lived.

② Experiencing Nature

By Alan Dyer

WITH INTRODUCTION BY
Robert Vint

Alan Dyer is Senior Lecturer in Environmental and Scientific Studies and Co-ordinator of Environmental Education in the faculty of Arts and Education at the University of Plymouth. He has wide experience of teaching and leading groups of all ages and backgrounds. His infectious enthusiasm for the natural world leads him into all areas of the curriculum.

Before children **explore** and **reflect** upon the beliefs and attitudes of different religions towards the natural world, it is recommended that they have direct experience of nature and the opportunity to explore and reflect upon their own responses to it. This forms the first part of REEP's learning cycle:

experience ——► explore ——► reflect ——► act

Introduction: The Nature of Spiritual Experience

The Alister Hardy Research Centre in Oxford has documented over four thousand accounts of spiritual experiences and in one of their publications points out that:

- most people, irrespective of whether or not they have any religious beliefs, have had spiritual experiences,
- such experiences are particularly common in childhood,
- they usually occur in relation to the natural world.

Here are some examples quoted in *Seeing the Invisible: A Study of Modern Religious Experiences* (Verena Tschudin, Arkana, available from AHRC research):

When I was about eleven years old I spent part of a summer holiday in the Wye Valley. Waking up very early one bright morning, before any of the household was about, I left my bed and went to kneel on the window-seat to look out over the curve which the river took just below the house. The trees between the house and the river – I was on a level with their topmost branches – were either poplars or silver birch, and green fields stretched away beyond the river to the far distance. The morning sunlight shimmered on the leaves of the trees and on the rippling surface of the river. The scene was very beautiful, and quite suddenly I felt myself on the verge of a great revelation. It was as if I had stumbled unwittingly on a place where I was not expected, and was about to be initiated into some wonderful mystery, something of indescribable significance. Then, just as suddenly, the feeling faded. But for the brief seconds while it lasted I had known that in some strange way I, the essential me – was a part of the trees, of the sunshine, and the river, that we all belonged to some great unity. I was left filled with exhilaration and exultation of spirit. This is one of the most memorable experiences of my life, of a quite different quality and greater intensity than the sudden lift of the spirit one may often feel when confronted with beauty in nature.

The first approach to a spiritual experience which I can remember must have taken place when I was five or six years old at the house where I was born and brought up. It was a calm, limpid summer morning and the early mist still lay in wispy wreaths among the valleys. The dew on the grass seemed to sparkle like iridescent jewels in the sunlight, and the shadows of the houses and trees seemed friendly and protective. In the heart of the child that I was there suddenly seemed to well up a deep and overwhelming sense of gratitude, a sense of unending peace and security which seemed to be part of the beauty of the morning, the love and protective and living presence which included all that I had ever loved and yet was something much more.

As a child (not younger than 6, not older than 8), I had an experience which nowadays I consider as kindred, if not identical, with those experiences related by Wordsworth in The Prelude [Bk. 1, lines 379–400]. The circumstances were: dusk, summertime, and I one of a crowd of grown-ups and children assembled round the shore of a large ornamental lake, waiting for full darkness before a firework display was to begin. A breeze stirred the leaves of a group of poplars just to my right; stirred, they gave a fluttering sound. There, then, I knew or felt or experienced – what? Incommunicable now, but then much more so. The sensations were of awe or wonder, and a sense of astounding beauty – at that moment in dusk – and the perception that it would have gone when it was dark and the fireworks began. And so it was. I remember exactly the place where the experience occurred and have since often revisited it, at various hours but nothing of quite the same kind (despite a host of intense experiences of different kinds since) happened again. That child of 6 or 7 or 8 knew nothing of Wordsworth or about mysticism or about religion.

We see in these descriptions by people unfamiliar with any religious vocabulary a recognition or experience of three things:

- a sense of oneness, belonging and unity with nature and its source,
- an awareness of revelation,
- a sense of a presence within and behind nature.

How Can Pupils Experience the World around Them?

The secret is, of course, to take the children to a beautiful natural place. Imagine it … a wondrous forest clearing studded with vibrant-coloured wild flowers, the air heavy with sweet scents and sparkling with the sounds of birds and insects, a view of the distant mountains and a glimpse of the sea, your children dancing and playing in the mists of a waterfall …

Yes, OK, back to reality – how many teachers can realistically take their pupils to such places regularly? We all know the arguments of cost, time, lack of access to nature, pressures of the curriculum and family life, the endless bureaucracy and so on. But in the end, intense experiences in the natural world will have a stronger and more lasting influence than any other learning tool.

If that 'nature' is a few flowers around a pond in an inner-city school playground, then the experience must be carefully crafted to make it unforgettable. All the clever and exciting activities that you will find in this and other books will lack any real meaning if not backed by memorable experiences in nature. In the classroom you can introduce, reinforce, recreate, simulate, record and process, but you cannot *really* give the children experience of the world around them. So, no matter where your school is located – country, inner city or suburb – start planning a visit to the natural world!

With careful planning and your own teacher's intuition *any* visit to the natural world should be a memorable experience. Even in the middle of a city a blindfold walk (described on page 19) can be a wonderful journey of discovery, but to make it really special you will probably need some help. Rachel Carson, in her book *The Sense of Wonder*, asks '... that the good fairy gives each new-born child a sense of wonder so indestructible that it lasts through life as an unfailing antidote to the boredom and disenchantment of later life.' She goes on to give a vitally important message to teachers and parents:

If a child is to keep alive his inborn sense of wonder without any such gift from the fairies, he needs the companionship of at least one adult who can share it, rediscovering the joy, excitement and mystery of the world we live in. Parents [and teachers – Ed.] often have a sense of inadequacy when confronted on the one hand with the eager, sensitive mind of a child and on the other with a world of complex physical nature, inhabited by a life so various and unfamiliar that it seems hopeless to reduce it to order and knowledge. In a mood of self defeat, they exclaim 'How can I possible teach my child about nature – why, I don't even know one bird from another!'

I sincerely believe that for the child, and for the parent seeking to guide her, it is not so important to **know** *as to* **feel** *... Once the emotions have been aroused – a sense of the beautiful, the excitement of the new and the unknown, a feeling of sympathy, pity, admiration or love – then we wish for knowledge about the object of our emotional response. Once found, it has lasting meaning.*

A very practical source of help are the books by Joseph Cornell which have inspired millions of teachers and parents the world over. The following text and outline of activities in this chapter have been taken from Joseph Cornell's best-selling books *Sharing Nature with Children* and *Sharing the Joy of Nature* with his full permission and blessing. He presents activities for the classroom as well as the natural world in a way that should excite any teacher without challenging their level of knowledge of the natural world. In the context of this book these activities are entirely appropriate as Joseph's work shows us how to experience more deeply the harmony and beauty of life. In *Sharing the Joy of Nature* he presents us with **Flow Learning**, which helps build awareness, cohesiveness and a variety of nature experiences to match your exact requirements.

Joseph Cornell's books:

Sharing Nature with Children
Sharing the Joy of Nature
Listening to Nature
Journey to the Heart of Nature

are published by Dawn Publications, Nevada City, California. They are available in the UK from Deep Books, London, SE8 5RT (Tel. 0171 232 2747).

Flow Learning

Learning with a Natural Flow

Flow Learning allows you to create an endless variety of nature experiences, each ideally matched to present circumstances and no two ever exactly alike. Although it's based on a few simple principles, it's not a rigid system of activities that you always have to do the same way. You can use Flow Learning with the games and activities from my books, and with any other resources you may know.

I've used Flow Learning successfully in sessions that lasted from 30 minutes to all day. I've used it indoors in rainy weather and outdoors in the sun. It's very flexible, because it gives you the freedom to respond appropriately to the needs of the moment. The goal of Flow Learning is to give everyone a genuinely uplifting experience of nature. After a successful Flow Learning session, each person feels a subtle, enjoyable new awareness of his oneness with nature and an increased empathy with all of life.

Outdoors, there are any number of distractions that can prevent your group from becoming aware of its surroundings. Aside from distractions like cars, machinery, and even human voices, they may be feeling cold, or they may be worried about personal problems. A great strength of Flow Learning is that it helps people free their attention so they can relax, have fun, and enjoy the natural world.

The strong central current of a river carries away the sluggish eddies that form along the river's banks. Similarly, when you introduce people to nature with playful activities that energize the body and mind, the high energy that the games develop washes away personal problems and moods. Freed from personal worries, their enthusiasm and attention can flow into new and fascinating experiences.

Experiential learning isn't a new idea. What's unique about Flow Learning is that it lays out the stages a person goes through to get into a frame of mind where deep, direct experiences are possible. It's a tool to help people become receptive to nature as quickly and efficiently as possible. Because it's based on human nature, it can be creatively applied anywhere – in the classroom and in our personal lives.

Joseph Cornell realized that there was a sequence for using games and activities that always seemed to work best, regardless of a group's age, its mood, or the physical setting. He became convinced that the reason people responded so well to this particular sequence was that it is in harmony with certain subtle aspects of human nature. He blended all the outdoor activities he had collected or created into a way of teaching which he called 'Flow Learning' – because it has four stages (see table overleaf) that flow from one into another in a smooth, natural way:

Stage 1: Awaken Enthusiasm
Stage 2: Focus Attention
Stage 3: Direct Experience
Stage 4: Share Inspiration

Stage 1: Awaken Enthusiasm

Without enthusiasm, you can never have a meaningful experience of nature. By enthusiasm, I'm not talking about wild-eyed, jumping-up-and-down excitement, but a calm, intense flow of personal interest and keen alertness. Without this kind of enthusiasm, we learn very little. As the name suggests, this stage is playful. Fun-filled games and activities create a lively flow of energy. Through shared fun, the Enthusiasm stage gives people a feeling of closeness with one another. It creates a base of alertness and enthusiasm on which you can build subtler, more meaningful learning experiences.

Flow Learning

Stage 1: **Awaken Enthusiasm**

Quality: Playfulness and alertness
Benefits:
- Builds on children's love of play.
- Creates an atmosphere of enthusiasm.
- A dynamic beginning gets everyone saying 'Yes!'
- Develops full alertness, overcomes passivity.
- Creates involvement.
- Gets attention (minimizes discipline problems).
- Develops rapport with the leader.
- Creates good group dynamics.
- Provides direction and structure.
- Prepares for later, more-sensitive activities.

Stage 2: **Focus Attention**

Quality: Receptivity
Benefits:
- Increases attention span.
- Deepens awareness by focusing attention.
- Positively channels enthusiasm generated in Stage 1.
- Develops observational skills.
- Calms the mind.
- Develops receptivity for more-sensitive nature experiences.

Stage 3: **Direct Experience**

Quality: Absorption
Benefits:
- People learn best by personal discovery.
- Gives direct, experiential, intuitive understanding.
- Fosters wonder, empathy, and love.
- Develops personal commitment to ecological ideals.

Stage 4: **Share Inspiration**

Quality: Idealism
Benefits:
- Clarifies and strengthens personal experiences.
- Builds on uplifted mood.
- Introduces inspiring role models.
- Gives peer reinforcement.
- Creates group bonding.
- Provides feedback for the leader.
- Leader can share inspiration with a receptive audience.

When you lead nature outings, it's extremely important to get off to a good start, because people generally decide within a few minutes whether they're going to have a good time. By starting with lively games, you're far more likely to get the group's whole-hearted participation. Many people resist anything new. To get them to participate enthusiastically in sensitive nature activities, you'll first have to convince them that they're going to have a good time – in other words, that in this case at least, 'new' is going to equal 'fun'. The first stage accomplishes this. Grown-ups and teenagers are more likely than young children to adopt a cool, wait-and-see stance, but I've seen the power of the Stage 1 games win over even very sceptical groups.

The attention-focusing effect of these playful games deflects potential discipline problems before they occur. The children become so engrossed in having fun that they have no time for mischief. The magical power of the first-stage games never ceases to amaze me. Focused attention creates an inner calmness and openness that allows us to experience nature directly, without the interference of static from the mind. As you become familiar with the games and gain experience with groups of varied ages, you'll find it increasingly easy to sense a group's needs and choose appropriate activities.

Awaken Enthusiasm Activities

A1. Bat and Moth

Get the group to form a circle about 5 metres across. Choose a player to be the bat and 3–5 others to be moths. Ask the bat and moths to come to the centre of the circle. Blindfold the bat and tell the players, 'Whenever the bat calls out "Bat!", all of the moths must call out "Moth!"'.

Bats find their way around by sending out high-pitched sounds that reflect like sonar. The bat tracks the moths by listening for their responses and trying to tag them. It takes good concentration to be a successful bat. So this game is good for developing concentration, especially when the bat must chase several moths at the same time. Add some excitement by bringing two bats into the circle at once. Encourage the bats to hunt as a team. I usually choose a tall bat and a short one, so they won't bang heads if they bump into each other.

A2. Owls and Crows

This is an excellent game for revising newly learned concepts and facts. Divide the group into two equal teams, the Owls and the Crows. Line the two teams facing each other, about half a metre apart. About 5 metres behind each team, draw a line for Base. The leader makes a statement aloud, and if the statement is true the Owls chase the Crows – trying to catch them before they reach their own Base. If the statement is false, the Crows chase the Owls. Anyone caught must join the other team. If the answer isn't obvious to the players, you'll find some of the Owls and Crows running towards each other, and others running back to their Bases. During the pandemonium, the leader should remain silent and neutral. When the action has calmed down, he can reveal the correct answer. Here are some sample statements: Sensory: 'The wind is coming from behind the Crows.' Conceptual: 'A deciduous tree keeps its leaves all year long.' Observational: (after showing them a leaf) 'The leaf had five points and five veins.' Identification: 'This seed comes from an oak tree.'

A3. What Animal Am I?

Mount some pictures of animals on cards and collect some clothes pegs. Peg a picture of an animal on the back of each participant. Don't let them see the picture.

Each person then mingles and asks someone else a question – the other person can only answer 'Yes', 'No' or 'I don't know'. Everyone keeps mingling and asking questions until they have discovered their animal. When they have discovered their animal they can peg the picture to their front. This game is a great ice-breaker – just add that each person should introduce themself before they ask a question.

A4. Animal Parts

This game is for groups of four or five children. Ask each group to select an animal then tell them that each group will have to imitate their animal. They are going to appear before a 'panel of experts' who will try to guess their identity on the basis of the movement and behaviour they act out. No noise is allowed, except what they can make with props (optional) such as a can with pebbles in it to mimic the rattle of a rattlesnake.

Give the groups about five minutes to work on the acts: 'Oh, no! A scorpion has eight legs – we'll all have to be legs! ... I can be the head, too, since I'm at the front, and my arms can be the pincers ... Okay, I'll be the tail, but I don't think I can hold it too long. You guys have to bend forward and hold onto each other to make the body. Ready?'

Stage 2: Focus Attention

Learning depends on focused attention – enthusiasm alone isn't enough. If our thoughts are scattered, we can't be dynamically aware of nature, or anything else. So we must bring our enthusiasm to a calm focus. If we give complete attention to what we're observing, we can see nature in fresh, new ways. At the close of the Enthusiasm stage, people are usually having lots of fun and feeling relaxed and enthusiastic. Now you can begin to bring that energy to a fine focus, with games that help people become calmly, enthusiastically attentive. The games of Stage 2 (Attention) help develop calmness and receptivity.

To free our attention for nature, we need to quiet our mind. But if you introduce quiet, sensitive activities too soon, many people will still be too restless to enjoy them. The Attention stage serves as a bridge between energetic, playful games and games that call for quiet, focused attention. The games of the Attention stage are simple but remarkably effective. Not only do they help people become more observant, they also help attune heart and mind to nature's beauty.

One of my favourite Attention activities is the Sounds Game. To play, you tell the group to sit, close their eyes and hold up their fists. Every time they hear a sound, they raise a finger. After a few minutes they can share descriptions of the sounds they heard. The game is short and sweet, but very effective for concentrating the participants' minds and settling the group after the Stage 1 activities. Another game which naturally follows this is the Sound Map (see page 17). Like the Sounds Game the Sound Map simply and naturally helps the players become more sensitive to the immediate environment. It is also interesting to follow this up with some art activities that try to describe sounds in shape or colour.

The Attention stage need not last long – 5–15 minutes is plenty. If the surroundings are really spectacular – thousands of waterfowl flying overhead at a nature reserve, for example – you might not have to use any Stage 2 (Attention) games at all. The magic of the environment will seize the group's attention, and your challenge will be the enjoyable one of helping them absorb the setting as fully as possible.

What do you do if you find yourself faced with the challenge of giving 30 children a meaningful experience of nature in a concrete inner-city playgound that has a single, scrawny tree? You may need to devote a lot of time to waking up their interest, before you can begin helping them to see the tree in new ways.

The important thing in Stage 2 is to be intensely aware of the group's level of *enthusiasm and receptivity. Ask yourself, 'Are they ready for more sensitive experiences yet?' If not, then ask, 'What other games can I use to raise their enthusiasm and focus their attention?'*

Focus Attention Activities

A5. **Sounds**

Ask the children to sit or lie on their backs and raise both fists. Each time a player hears a new sound they raise a finger. Share your findings. Follow this with ...

A6. **Sound Map**

Give each member of the group a plain postcard with an X drawn in the centre. Tell the players the card is a map, and that the X shows where they're sitting. When they hear a sound, they should make a mark on the card that 'describes' the sound – for example, wavy lines indicating wind, or a musical note for a bird's song. The mark should indicate the sound's distance and direction.

Ask everyone to find a special 'listening place' quickly, so that some aren't walking around while others are already listening. I usually give the group one minute to find a spot and tell them to stay in the same spot until the end of the game. Giving the players enough time to disperse fairly widely will ensure a diversity of sound maps and greater interest in sharing. How long you should play depends on the group's age, attention span, and how well-supplied the environment is with sounds. A good basic guideline is 10 minutes for adults, 5 minutes for children. I like to call the group back together by imitating a natural sound and ask them to share their maps with each other. Ask them what sounds they've heard and which sounds they liked best. Why did they like those particular sounds? Which sounds had they never heard before? How did they represent the sounds in the drawing?

A good follow-up back in class is to play various sounds and let the group draw or paint them.

A7. **Un-Nature Trail**

This game is played primarily to introduce the concepts of camouflage (protective colouring) and adaptation. Choose a 10–20 metre section of footpath and place along it about 20 human-made objects. Some of them should stand out brightly, like plastic figures or balloons. Others should blend with their surroundings, and therefore be more difficult to pick out. Keep the number of objects you've planted secret. The children walk over the section of trail one at a time, with intervals between them, trying to spot (not pick up) as many of the objects as they can. When they reach the end of the trail, they whisper in your ear how many they saw. Tell them a rough percentage of how many of the objects they saw and if they didn't see them all tell them to start again and have another look. End the game with a discussion of the ways colour camouflage helps animals. Then go on a search for some camouflaged animals (insects, spiders, etc.).

A8. **Barefoot Walk**

A fine way to encourage people to slow down is to take them on a barefoot walk. It's amazing how quiet and attentive even large groups become when they have to pay attention to where they're putting their feet! There is a wonderful quality to the experience of watching animals close-up in the wild, entering into their world quietly and unobtrusively. There's none of the panic that accompanies the usual noisy human intrusion into their habitat. Wild animals going about their activities are serene and poised. Watching them stimulates feelings of kinship with the animal world. A slow pace encourages the walkers to pause and look around, increasing their chances of seeing wildlife. If you plan the walk for sunrise or sunset, more animals will be moving about. The calm, reflective atmosphere at dawn and dusk helps the group tune in to the spirit of quiet observation. An entertaining way to introduce the game is to teach the players to walk quietly, Indian-fashion. Ask them to take off their shoes and socks. Then ask them to take a very slow, short step forward, coming down gently on the outside of the descending foot and rolling it inward slowly until the foot is level. At this point, the sole of the foot should be only lightly touching the ground. Before shifting full weight onto the lead foot, they should feel whether there are any twigs, leaves, or other objects that might make a noise. If there aren't, tell them to bring their weight slowly onto the lead foot. Tell them that by taking short steps they'll have better balance and thus will feel free to give more attention to looking for animals.

The leader should check the route of the walk beforehand to remove any obvious hazards.

A9. Animals, Animals!

Place animal picture cards on the ground and have the players choose the animal they want to imitate. Tell the players to keep their animal's identity secret. Have the players act out the animal's typical behaviour, one player at a time. Each player holds the pose of their animal for a few seconds, then begins moving like the animal but not making any sounds. In large groups, 5–10 volunteers can perform at the same time, if you prefer.

Animals, Animals! is a good game for helping people develop deeper rapport with animals. If you play Animals, Animals! at a zoo or a farm be sure to take advantage of opportunities to let the players see real, live animals. If you tell the group you're going to ask them to play the animals later, it'll whet their interest in observing them closely. They'll learn more, and it'll also increase their empathy for 'their' animal.

Stage 3: Direct Experience

Although Stage 3 (Direct Experience) and Stage 2 (Focus Attention) are similar, they differ in the greater power of the Direct Experience games to involve people directly in nature. For example, shutting off people's sense of sight makes them experience their surroundings in fresh ways. Each of the Direct Experience activities is designed to intensify one or more sense-element of the nature experience.

You can give people deeply inspiring experiences of nature even in public parks. All it takes is a little creativity. The Flow Learning technique was developed with difficult situations like these in mind. If it's raining and you have to come indoors, you can still use all the stages of Flow Learning. There are many activities that give the participants enjoyable 'nature-experiences' with the help of the imagination.

Direct experiences of nature enable us to enter fully into the spirit of the natural world. They help us discover a deep, inner sense of belonging and understanding. If people are to develop a love and concern for the earth, they need to have these direct experiences; otherwise their knowing remains remote and theoretical and never touches them deeply. After a deep, direct experience of nature, the mind is quiet and receptive, fully absorbed in the event. Direct experience awakens a sense of wonder. It enables us to reach out and feel other realities.

With direct-experience learning, we stretch our awareness to include the surrounding world. Only with such empathy can we truly begin to know nature. Thoreau said, 'it is only by forgetting yourself that you draw near to God.' This is just as true of nature. In the Stage 3 games, people expand beyond their own little worlds. They emerge from the narrow cocoon of self to discover a richer, larger world, filled with harmony. As we gradually focus our attention, we become more aware of what we're seeing, hearing, touching, smelling, and receiving through intuition. With calm attention, we can enter more sensitively into the rhythm and flow of nature all around us.

Direct Experience Activities

NB Most of these are suitable for urban areas as well as the countryside.

A10. Camera
Camera is one of the most powerful and enjoyable activities in this series of games. In a simple and natural way, it quiets distracting thoughts and restlessness and frees the attention for absorbing nature with unobstructed clarity.

Ask the players to pair off in twos. One player takes the role of photographer, and the other plays the camera. The camera keeps his eyes closed until the photographer sees an interesting subject for a picture. The photographer then taps the camera on the shoulder, and the camera opens its shutter (eyes) until the photographer taps again signalling to close the shutter (3–5 seconds is a good exposure time). Encourage the photographers to be creative in choosing and framing pictures, choosing unusual camera angles, panning the camera during exposure, and taking close ups. After everyone has played both roles, give each player a 3 x 5 index card and tell them, 'Remember one of the pictures you took when you played camera. Develop it by drawing it, and give it to the photographer.' If some players groan self-consciously about their lack of artistic talent, tell them they can blame the quality of their pictures on the photographer!

A11. Blindfold Trail
On a blindfold trail a rope-guided group of travellers roam through lands full of strange sounds, mysterious smells, and interesting textures. Most travellers can hardly wait to retrace their steps through this enchanted land with eyes open. Your trail can be set up just about anywhere – but try to find an area that offers a variety of experiences. Decide which side of the rope the children will walk on and give the children some idea of how to explore the trail, so they won't just run through it. Encourage them to be silent as they explore.

A12. Blind Walk
It's very simple to organize and lead a blind walk. Form pairs, with mixed adults and children, or children together. Each pair decides who'll be leader and guides his partner along any route that looks attractive – being very careful to watch out for logs, low branches, and so on. The leader also guides his blind partner within range of interesting sounds and smells and touches.

A13. Meet a Tree
The players find a partner and one player blindfolds the other and leads her through the forest to a tree, then helps her explore the tree. Specific suggestions work best: 'Rub your hand on the bark. Is the tree alive? Are there plants growing on it?' When they've finished exploring, the first player leads his partner back to the start by a new route. Remove the blindfold and ask the player to try to find the tree. Suddenly, what was a forest becomes a collection of very individual trees!

A14. Caterpillar Walk
Take your children to a secluded, secret spot. After blindfolding them, arrange the children in a line, caterpillar-fashion with each child placing their hands on the

shoulders of the child ahead. Tell them that as you lead them along they are to listen to the sounds and feel their surroundings as completely as they can. Make frequent stops along the way at points of interest such as unusual trees and rocks, or to smell a fragrant flower or bush. The more variety there is along the route, the better. To add variety, walk on and off paths, walk through clumps of bracken, or go in and out sunny forest clearings.

When you have gone as far as you think is appropriate, remove the blindfolds. The children must now try to find their way back along the route to the starting point. Before they turn back ask them to draw a picture or map of what they think the course and areas we passed through look like. This helps them translate into pictures the sounds, smells and touches they've experienced. Caution: blind caterpillars more than six segments long quickly become entangled and hard to manage.

Stage 4: Share Inspiration

At the end of Stage 3, the players feel calmly exhilarated. They're in the right mood for activities that bring out nature's heart-warming, beautiful, and uplifting side. Now is a good time to introduce stories that portray the noble ideals of the great naturalists and also to let people talk about their earlier experiences while playing the games. Sharing reinforces the players' sense of wonder and draws the group together.

The simple activities of the Inspiration stage also bring a sense of closure and wholeness to the programme. The leader finds out what people have been thinking and feeling while they've played the games, and this stimulates lots of good ideas for leading future sessions. The games and activities of the Inspiration stage are very simple. You could ask people to mime something they've seen or felt during your time together. If the group has become close and has experienced beautiful moments together, the sharings can be very powerful.

After leading a Flow Learning session, I sat at sundown with a group at the edge of a vast marsh. We watched the sunset for a long time, then did the mime activity just after the sun had gone down. A twelve-year-old girl climbed to the top of the bank, turned toward us, and clasped her hands above her head, holding her arms in a circle. She stood there a moment smiling, then slowly walked backward down the other side of the bank. Her rendition of the sunset was so perfect that it touched everyone, reminding us of the beautiful moment we'd shared.

Experience opens up deeper awareness. In Still Hunting (see page 22), the player remains very, very still while nature returns to its normal routine all around. Let's imagine that you're still hunting and birds land very close in a tree overhead. By remaining still, you begin to feel a kind of breathless oneness with life all around you, almost as if you were blending into the scene and experiencing life through the birds, the grass, and the waving branches of the trees. In that stillness, you can sometimes feel a great, bursting joy or a deep, calm happiness, or an overwhelming sense of the beauty or power of creation. Nature is always inspiring, and it's only our restless minds that keep us from being more often joyfully aware of this.

A leader can help a group deepen its inspiration by telling stories about nature that uplift and inspire, or by telling stories from the lives of the great naturalists and conservationists. I call the fourth stage Sharing Inspiration, because sharing strengthens and clarifies our own deep experiences.

Share Inspiration Activities

A15. **Silent Sharing Walk**
OF ALL the activities in this section, the Silent Sharing Walk is potentially the most powerful. Walk in silence, abandoning words and trappings of civilization – shoes,

for example, and synthetic clothing that makes such un-nature-like noises. The silence and harmony of this activity, especially at dawn or dusk, create an awareness that we are sharing the world with all living things. Because the walk requires sensitivity and subtle application, I offer it only to children who I feel will be receptive and able to enter into the spirit of silent sharing. When a person feels a sense of unity with the world, his feelings of harmony with other people are intensified, too. Through watching nature in silence, we discover within ourselves feelings of relatedness with whatever we see – plants, animals, stones, earth and sky.

A16. **Nature Meditations**

Before playing Nature Meditations, you'll need to write inspiring nature-related sayings on index cards, one saying per card. Each saying should have an accompanying activity that helps the reader translate the thought into direct experience. Avoid sayings that are too abstract and philosophical. You'll find 30 quotations with suggested activities in Joseph Cornell's book *Listening to Nature*. Some examples are given at the end of this section (see pages 22–23).

A beautiful setting helps the players enter into the spirit of their quotation. It's all right for players to use quotations of their own, and it's okay to give the same quotation to more than one player. Allow 10–15 minutes for quiet reflection, then call the group together and ask them to sit in a circle and talk about their experiences.

A17. **Expanding Circles**

You cannot perceive beauty but with a serene mind.

H.D. THOREAU

Find a place with a panoramic view and an interesting foreground. Sit down, close your eyes, and become aware of your own body. Then open your eyes and extend your awareness beyond your body just a few feet to include the nearby grasses, rocks, and insects. Feel yourself moving and becoming alive in them. Try to feel that you are in everything you see, as much as you are in your own body. Continue to gradually extend your visual awareness in stages until it finally reaches the distant horizon and the vast blue sky. All the while, keep the awareness of yourself in the things closest to you, as well as all the way out to the horizon.

A18. **Stillness Meditation**

The still mind of the sage is a mirror of heaven and earth.

CHUANG TZU

Sit up with a straight back and calmly gaze at a beautiful scene before you. Observe the natural flow of your breath. Do not control it in any way! Each time you inhale, think 'Still'. Each time you exhale, think 'Ness'. Repeating 'Still ... Ness' with each complete breath helps focus the mind and prevents your attention from wandering from the present moment.

During the pauses between inhalation and exhalation, stay in the present moment, calmly observing whatever is in front of you. If thoughts of the past or future disturb your mind, just calmly, patiently bring your attention back to what is before you, and to repeating 'Still ... Ness' with your breathing.

Listening to Nature

These additional meditations and activities to focus the mind would be suitable for teachers or older pupils.

A19. **Walking and Feeling Yourself in All**

Wonderful how completely everything in wild nature fits into us, as if truly part and parent of us. The sun shines not on us, but in us. The river flows not past, but through us, thrilling, tingling, vibrating every fibre and cell of the substance of our bodies, making them glide and sing.

JOHN MUIR

As you walk, feel yourself in every natural sound and movement. Feel in everything around you the oneness of life.

A20. **Still Hunting**

I think I could turn and live with the animals, they are so placid and self-contained.

WALT WHITMAN

Choose a place where there's likely to be frequent animal activity, sit motionless, and blend into the natural surroundings. Wait quietly and observe the animals as they go about their normal harmonious activity.

Go for a walk and silently repeat one of these quotations, reflecting upon its meaning.

*Never a day passes
but that I do myself the honour
to commune with some of
nature's varied forms.*

G.W. CARVER

If you live it enough anything will talk with you.

G.W. CARVER

*Holy Earth Mother
the trees and all nature
are witnesses
of your thoughts and deeds.*

WINNEBAGO INDIANS

*With beauty before me,
May I walk
With beauty behind me,
May I walk
With beauty above me,
May I walk
With beauty around me,
May I walk
Wandering on a trail of beauty,
Lively I walk.*

NAVAHO INDIANS

The best and most beautiful things in the world cannot be seen or even touched. They must be felt with the heart.

HELEN KELLER

The rare moment is not the moment when there is something worth looking at but the moment when we are capable of seeing.

JOSEPH WOOD KRUTCH

My heart is tuned to the quietness
that the stillness of nature inspires.

H.I. KHAN

Find a quiet place where you can be alone. Listen to the sounds around you. Listen also for the silences between the sounds. When your mind wanders, reread the above saying. It will help bring you back to the present moment.

> *The birds of the air are my brothers*
> *All flowers my sisters,*
> *The trees are my friends.*
> *All living creatures,*
> *Mountains and streams,*
> *I take unto my care.*
> *For this green earth is our mother,*
> *Hidden in the sky is the Spirit above*
> *I share one life with all who are here*
> *To everyone I give my love,*
> *To everyone I give my love.*

After experiencing the natural world for themselves, children will be ready to start exploring and reflecting upon religious attitudes towards the natural world using the activities in Chapters 3–7.

Buddhism and the Natural World

By Kevin Fossey

Kevin Fossey is Head of the Dharma School, the only primary school in the UK to provide Buddhist-based education. He has experience of deputy headship and headship of four mainstream schools and of teacher training at Brighton University and with the Tibetan Govenment in Exile. Kevin practises Tibetan Buddhism with the Maitrikara Sangha and he is the REEP trainer for Buddhism.

> **Important**
>
> When exploring religious beliefs and practices with your class, remember:
>
> - To use non-inclusive language. That is, use phrases such as 'Buddhists believe that ...', 'Buddhism teaches that humans should ...', 'It is important to Buddhists that/to ...'.
>
> - That within world faiths there are significant variations in both belief and practice. Although contributors to this book focus on widely followed teachings (unless stated otherwise), these may receive different emphasis or interpretation from different groups within that faith community.

Buddhist Beliefs and Values

Activities B1, B2 and B3 (pages 28–29) are designed to help children explore and reflect on aspects of these **teachings about the world**.

Teachings about the World

The Buddha taught that the idea that we exist as isolated entities is an illusion. All living things are interrelated; and we are part of that interconnectedness and do not have autonomous existence. Buddha came to understand that respect for life and the natural world is essential. By living simply one can be in harmony with other creatures and learn to appreciate the interconnectedness of all that lives. This simplicity of life involves developing care and respect for our environment and relating to the world with awareness and responsive perception. It enables us to enjoy without possessing, and to benefit each other without manipulation.

Buddha also taught that everything is impermanent; and that we change as much as everything else in the natural world. Change is the very essence of nature – we are not solid and permanent entities but are constantly changing.

Many Buddhist teachers emphasize the natural relationship between ecology and Buddhism. However, we cannot begin to change the environment if individuals are not in a state of equilibrium. So often the mind and heart are like untamed tigers rampaging through our daily lives. Motivated by desire, grasping and bewilderment the untamed mind and heart pursue what they want – lashing out at anything standing in their way. Therefore, efforts to change the environment must begin with ourselves. Buddha taught a path from selfishness to generosity, from ignorance to wisdom, from hatred to loving-kindness. Openness, mindfulness, compassion and wisdom are the very essence of Buddhism.

When we respect the environment, then nature will be good to us. When our hearts are good, then the sky will be good to us. The trees are like our mother and father, they feed us, nourish us, and provide us with everything; fruit, leaves, the branches, the trunk. They give us food and satisfy many of our needs.

MAHA GHOSANANDA, THE LEADING MONK IN CAMBODIA

Like the Buddha, we too should look around us and be observant, because everything in the world is ready to teach us. With even a little wisdom we will be able to see clearly through the ways of the world. We will come to understand that everything in the world is a teacher. Trees and vines, for example, can all reveal the true nature of reality.

AJAHN CHAH, FROM THE FOREST SANGHA, THAILAND

Vietnamese Zen monk Thich Nhat Hanh has written extensively about the joy of 'living in the moment'. For example:

Our true home is the present moment. To live in the present moment is a miracle ... It is a miracle to walk on the green Earth in the present moment, to appreciate the peace and beauty that are available now.

> *Breathing in, I know I'm breathing in,*
> *Breathing out, I know*
> *as the in-breath grows deep,*
> *the out-breath grows slow.*
> *Breathing in makes me calm.*
> *Breathing out makes me ease.*
> *With the in-breath, I smile.*
> *With the out-breath, I release.*
> *Breathing in, there is only the present moment.*
> *Breathing out is a wonderful moment.*

Spiritual Teachings

Activities B4, B5, B6, B7, B8 and B9 (pages 29–32) are designed to help children explore and reflect on aspects of these **spiritual teachings**.

Buddhist teachers have often reminded people of the importance of living in tune with nature, to respect all life, to make time for meditation practice, to live simply and use nature as a spiritual force.

Meditation has come to mean different things to different people. Fundamentally, though, it involves allowing the mind to settle and remain in its natural state, free from grasping to dualistic concepts, i.e. free from the ideas of subject, object and action. It uses a variety of techniques such as awareness of breath, being in tune with nature, visualization, prayer and mantra recitation, but all these simply serve to help the mind free itself from its five main obstacles – passion, aggression, ignorance, jealousy and pride – and through this allow its own natural wisdom to shine through. Meditation combined with developing openness and warmth of heart in everyday existence can lead to a transformation of one's life and an awakening of the potential for enlightenment.

The monks and nuns living at the Chithurst Buddhist Monastery in Hampshire use simplicity and periods of retreat and solitude to give the opportunity of deepening, refining and strengthening the mind. The forest has its own rhythms and after a few days the metabolism and sleeping patterns adjust and the senses begin to sharpen to the new and unfamiliar setting. When not having any of the comforts of life such as gas, electricity and artificial light our ears and noses begin to play a more important role. Living close to nature can be a very healing experience – there are few activities and distractions. This teaches the truth of the notion of impermanence – changes in the sounds of animals, changing texture and appearance of trees, subtle changes in forest and land, subtle changes in your own mind. By being mindful about the daily routine one pays attention to the flow of life – to see nature as a positive, joyful, spiritual force.

Moral Teachings

Activity B10 (page 32) is designed to help children explore and reflect on aspects of these **moral teachings**.

Buddhism advocates a simple, gentle, non-aggressive attitude towards nature. Craving and greed bring unhappiness – our demands for material possessions will never be satisfied and no government can fulfil all our desires for security. If we can conquer greed and desire we can start to be at peace with those around us.

Buddha taught that the way to enlightenment is through understanding the Four Noble Truths, and this understanding can serve as a framework for spiritual practice.

The Four Noble Truths

The First Truth teaches that all conditioned existence is pervaded by suffering. This reality of dissatisfaction must be acknowledged before we can begin to free ourselves from it.

The Second Truth states that all suffering arises out of causes, the three principal causes being greed (craving), hatred and delusion (ignorance).

The Third Truth says simply that when the causes are abandoned, the suffering will cease. When we become selfless persons, the fruit will be peace and happiness.

The Fourth Truth shows the way to attain this, the path we can follow to help us and all beings towards liberation and wisdom. The way pioneered by the Buddha is open to all – the way of wisdom, discipline and meditation, called the Noble Eightfold Path.

The Noble Eightfold Path
Here 'Right' means what is appropriate.

Wisdom
- **Right Understanding** (seeing the world as it is, in terms of the Four Noble Truths)
- **Right Thought** (growth of unselfishness and compassion)

Morality
- **Right Speech** (truthfulness, gentle and useful speech)
- **Right Action** (action in harmony with the Five Precepts – see below – and founded on love and compassion)
- **Right Livelihood** (avoiding occupations that cause harm or injustice, and choosing one which is beneficial to others)

Meditation
- **Right Effort** (to avoid negative thoughts and encourage positive)
- **Right Mindfulness** (attentiveness and awareness)
- **Right Concentration** (training the mind in the stages of meditation)

Our minds can so often be hyperactive demanding new distractions, making plans, always living in the future, not here and now in the present moment. Buddhist teachings encourage us to be more aware of our thoughts, actions, feelings and emotions, to move away from self-centredness, to share wealth more, to be responsible for ourselves and others, agreeing to live simply and help decrease the suffering in the world.

The Buddha commended frugality as a virtue in its own right. Skilful living avoids waste and we should try to recycle as much as we can. For Buddhists, the Five Moral

Precepts are important in forming attitudes of mind and guidance for living. Buddhists are encouraged to undertake a rule of training, the **Five Precepts**, to refrain from:

- harming and killing living beings;
- taking what is not freely given;
- misuse of senses, e.g. over-indulgence;
- wrong speech (gossiping, telling lies);
- taking drugs or drink that impair clarity of mind.

By starting to look at ourselves we may come to appreciate that the real solution to the environmental crisis begins with us.

Visions of the Future

Activities B11 and B12 (pages 33–34) are designed to help children explore and reflect on aspects of these **visions of the future**.

His Holiness the Dalai Lama has written and spoken at length on the need to learn to live in harmony and peace with each other and with nature. Nations and individuals have become increasingly interdependent and we have to develop the notion of universal responsibility. In our global family what happens in one part of the world can affect us all. In the words of His Holiness, 'peace can only last where human rights are respected, where people are fed and where nations and individuals are free ... Inner peace is the key; if you have inner peace, the external problems do not affect your deep sense of peace and tranquillity'.

Buddhism teaches that peace begins within each one of us and that we should be encouraged to work together. His Holiness has a dream that the entire Tibetan plateau should become a 'Zone of Peace' where humanity and nature can live in peace and harmony together. In his Nobel Peace Prize Lecture, His Holiness outlined the following key elements of the proposed Zone of Ahimsa (non-violence):

- The entire Tibetan plateau would be demilitarized.
- The manufacture, testing and stockpiling of nuclear weapons and other armaments on the Tibetan plateau would be prohibited.
- The Tibetan plateau would be transformed into the world's largest natural park or biosphere. Strict laws would be enforced to protect wildlife and plant life; the exploitation of natural resources would be carefully regulated so as not to damage relevant ecosystems; and a policy of sustainable development would be adopted in populated areas.
- The manufacture and use of nuclear power and other technologies which produce hazardous waste would be prohibited.
- Natural resources and policy would be directed towards the active promotion of peace and environmental protection. Organizations dedicated to the furtherance of peace and to the protection of all forms of life would find a hospitable home in Tibet.
- The establishment of international and regional organizations for the promotion and protection of human rights would be encouraged in Tibet.

Buddhist monasteries and Dharma centres (for sharing the Dharma, or Truth, taught by Buddha) will continue to provide a place of sanctuary and peace in the midst of the speed of the modern age. As more and more people understand that increased wealth does not necessarily mean increased happiness and that our planet cannot sustain the current demands made upon it, members of the human race are reflecting and seeking new ways of living. All faiths have incredibly precious and important teachings to offer; perhaps the development of the four boundless qualities in Buddhism – loving-kindness, compassion, joy (delight in the well-being of others) and equanimity (impartiality) – is a good starting-point for the future.

Buddhism Activities

Several activities included in chapters on other faiths could be adapted for use in units of work on Buddhism. These are asterisked in the Index of Activities on pages 112–113.

A range of introductory activities designed to help children respond to and reflect on the natural world appear in Chapter 2 (pages 15–23).

Activity B1
Interconnections

Age range
9–11 years

Time required
75 minutes

Location
Indoors

Resources
Felt-tips, crayons or paint, paper for posters

Objective

To examine our own personal responsibility for environmental pollution.

Procedure

1. Brainstorm 'What may be meant by "external" environmental pollution?' Ask for examples. These may include: destruction of the rainforests, the greenhouse effect, chemical spillage, volume of car traffic, litter, dirty rivers and seas.

2. Next move on to brainstorm 'What may be meant by "internal" environmental pollution?' Ask for (or give) some examples. These may include: overeating, lack of exercise or respect for our bodies, taking harmful substances such as drugs, alcohol or cigarettes. Encourage the children also to look more deeply at how emotions such as anger, jealousy, greed, desire, craving or aggression can cause environmental pollution.

3. The two parts of the question can then be merged to ask whether environmental pollution comes from 'inside' or 'outside'. Before we blame everyone else for causing pollution, shouldn't we examine our own actions and thoughts very carefully?

4. Ask the children to design a poster showing the connections between 'external' and 'internal' environmental pollution.

Activity B2
Impermanance in Nature

Age range
8–11 years

Time required
30 minutes

Location
Access to school garden, wild area, park or countryside

Resources
Pencils, paper

Objective

To explore Buddhist teachings of impermanence or interdependence by looking at how everything changes, everything is impermanent: i.e. mountains, movements of continents, birth/death, cycle of the year, snowflakes or seasons.

Procedure

1. Hold an introductory discussion with the children about the Buddha's teaching on impermanence: that everything is always changing.

2. Give the children 10 minutes to find something in the garden or grounds that is permanent and will last for ever.

3. Discuss findings.

4. Ask the children to make observational drawings working with materials in a state of change, i.e. leaves in different stages of decay, appearance of some trees at different times of year, before and after a haircut.

Activity B3
Webbing

Age range
Can be adapted
to suit ages
6–11 years

Time required
20–30 minutes

Location
Indoors

Resources
Large ball of string

Objective

To explore interconnections – how everything is interrelated.

Procedure

1. Sit the children in a circle. The teacher or leader stands in the circle, near the edge, holding the ball of string.

2. Hold a discussion on the following lines:

'Who can name something that grows in the school garden?'
'Tree!' Give the end of the string to the child who said this.
'Is there an animal around here that may live in the tree?'
'Squirrel!' That child holds on to the string further up.
'What do squirrels eat?'...

Continue the discussion, connecting children with string as the relationships of their answers to those of the rest of the group emerge. Bring in different elements such as animals, soil, water and so on until the entire circle of children is strung together in a symbol of the web of life.

3. To show how each of us individually is important to the whole community, 'take away' one member of the web, e.g. suppose a gardener cuts down the tree. To represent the tree falling, the child who said 'Tree!' tugs on the string; anyone else who feels the tug from the tree gives a tug. This continues until every individual is shown to be affected by the death of the tree.

Discussion points

Using this activity as a starting-point, the interrelated aspects of food chains and living chains can be discussed. The activity also helps children to appreciate the changes in the natural world going on around them. Flowers grow, bloom and fade. Rocks and mountains may look strong and impermanent, so we think that they will always be there, but they will change. What we do to the web of life we do to ourselves. We as individuals can have an effect on our environment and our decision-making also reflects on our environment.

Activity B4
Contemplative Exercise

Age range
7–11 years

Time required
15 minutes

Location
Park, wild garden
or countryside

Resources
None

Objective

To develop a greater awareness of surroundings and feelings.

Procedure

1. Whilst on a visit to the park or countryside, take some time out to encourage the children to sit quietly and close their eyes, perhaps near a beautiful view, a river, a tree or a hedge. Just ask the children to sit quietly for a while and note mentally what they hear and feel.

2. After a couple of moments encourage them to open their eyes and discuss with them what they noticed about their surroundings and what feelings they experienced.

3. Ask the children how they feel now and whether they can remember how they felt before, e.g. happy, fidgety, sad, interested, bored, peaceful, angry.

Activity B5
A Special Area

Age range
Can be adapted for
ages 4–11 years

Time required
Will depend on
children's responses
in initial discussion

Location
Outdoors or indoors

Resources
Will depend on
children's responses
in initial discussion

Objective

To develop appreciation, respect and care for a 'special' area. To give children responsibility and ownership of the area.

Procedure

1. Discuss with the children the idea of having a 'special' area in the classroom or the school grounds. What might make the area special? What would the children be able to contribute to making the area special? Where could the place be?

2. After this discussion help the children create a special area in the classroom or in the school grounds. Give the children ownership of the area by discussing with them the kinds of objects, flowers, plants they would place in the special area and begin to develop it.

Activity B6
Making Friends with My Body

Age range
6–11 years

Time required
10 minutes

Location
Indoors

Resources
None

Objective

To enable children to become more aware of their bodies and how the parts relate to each other.

Preparation

Before starting this activity take some time to practise some stilling exercises. Encourage the children to sit absolutely still for one minute. Ask them to try not to move at all – not even one tiny bit. It is useful to choose different signals for the beginning and the end of the exercise (such as 'tings' of a bell or cymbal). (See page 108 for resources on stilling and meditation.)

Procedure

1. Ask the children to sit and close their eyes. Ask them to sit quietly for a few moments then tell them:

'Think about your big toe, waggle it and it gives you a smile. Return the smile. Think about your thumb, bend it and it gives you a smile. Return the smile. Think about your stomach, breathe in and out, it smiles at you. Return the smile. Think about your nose, move it gently, it gives you a smile. Return the smile....'

Continue, using as many parts of the body as you wish, finishing with:

'Now open your eyes and smile at your nearest neighbour.'

2. This activity can be linked to the notion that in order to be kind to others it is important to be aware of ourselves, our bodies and our impact on others. An additional discussion point might be: 'Is it possible to see a human group as if they are parts of a body?'

Activity B7
Making Friends with Ourselves and Our Neighbours

Age range
Can be adapted to suit ages 4–11 years

Time required
10 minutes

Location
Indoors

Resources
None

Objective

To enable children to develop positive feelings towards themselves and others. To explore Buddhist teachings about caring for all living beings.

Preparation

Before beginning the activity undertake some preparatory stilling work. (See page 108 for resources on stilling and meditation.)

Procedure

1. Ask the children to sit and close their eyes. Tell them, 'Imagine a wonderful cascading waterfall of light is coming from above your head and flows through your head and throughout your body, your arms, your legs, your feet, rays of cascading light everywhere. Now your body is filled with light – a beautiful clear light. Imagine the light is now moving towards your tummy button. All the light throughout your body is moving, gently, slowly but purposefully towards your tummy. In the middle of your tummy button the light is concentrated in a ball, a very powerful ball no bigger than a penny. Send this light out to members of your family, then to your friends – to all the people you love. Now think about the people you have difficulty with, send them this light, your love as if you are shining like the sun. Open your eyes, try to hold that feeling and smile at your neighbours.'

The length and detail of this meditation will depend on the age and receptivity of the children. Leave periods of silence after each sentence.

2. This links to Buddhist teachings that people should care for all living beings – including those they have difficulty with.

Although this activity can be used as a 'Buddhist' meditation, it is not really 'religious', and can be attempted by anyone, of any religious faith or none.

Activity B8
Learning from Trees

Age range
8–11 years

Time required
45 minutes

Location
Access to some local trees

Resources
Pencils, paper

Objective

To develop awareness of the importance and interconnectedness of all living things.

Procedure

1. Ask the children to sit under a tree for a while and reflect upon it – to touch it, hold it, stroke it, hug it.

2. Ask questions such as: What animals and insects might live in the tree? What shelter does it provide? How did you feel about the tree and what did you learn from it? Why are trees important? What can be made from a tree? What does a tree give (e.g. home for animals/birds/insects, branches for fires, nuts/acorns, blossom, wood for furniture, violins, sculpture and paper)?

3. Distribute paper and pencils and ask the children to draw a web to show how trees support life.

Activity B9
The Magic of Patience

Age range
7–11 years

Time required
60 minutes

Location
Indoors

Objective

To reflect on patience and loving-kindness.

Resources

The Magic of Patience, a book in a Jataka Tales series (Dharma Publishing, ISBN 0 89800 189 7), or *The Patient Buffalo* from *Twenty Jataka Tales* (retold by Noor Inayat Khan, East West Publications, ISBN 0 85692 141 6) – both available through book shops or from Wisdom Books, 402 Hoe Street, London E17 9AA, pencils, paper

Background information

The Jataka Tales were first told by the Buddha over two thousand years ago. They celebrate the power of action motivated by compassion, love, wisdom and kindness. They teach that everything people think and do profoundly affects the quality of their lives.

Procedure

1. Read *The Magic of Patience* or *The Patient Buffalo* to the children.

2. Talk about the story with the children. Questions might include:

- What sorts of things 'count' as kindness?
- Can you share with us what arouses kindness in you?
- What kinds of behaviour by other people make you happy?
- What kinds of behaviour upset you?
- Why may it be helpful and useful for us to experience difficult, negative behaviour from other people? That is, if people are gentle and kind to us all the time, how can we develop patience?
- What is the use of patience? What do we do if we are not patient?

3. Encourage the children to write their own Jataka Tale. It should include animals and the theme of developing patience and kindness.

Activity B10
The Five Precepts

Age range
9–11 years

Time required
60 minutes

Location
Indoors

Resources
Crayons, paints, felt-tips, paper for posters

Objective

To explore the relevance of the Five Precepts in the modern world.

Procedure

1. Discuss with the children the meaning and significance of the Five Precepts (see page 27). Perhaps raise the issue that we can cause suffering unintentionally through what we buy or what we dispose of. This can be linked to major environmental issues such as vegetarianism, road building, consumerism, self-centredness, greed and craving, loving-kindness and compassion.

2. Children could design a poster illustrating one of the Five Precepts.

Activity B11
Some Case Studies

Age range
8–11 years

Time required
60 minutes

Location
Indoors

Resources
Infomation on projects being undertaken by the Buddhist community such as those outlined here, available from Kevin Fossey, The Dharma School, The White House, Ladies Mile Road, Patcham, Brighton BN1 8TB Telephone: 01273 502055

Objective

To understand some of the developments within the Buddhist community aimed at improving the environment.

Case studies

Buddhists all over the world are engaged in a number of practical activities aimed at improving our environment – both physically and emotionally. Outlined here are three projects which may make interesting case studies:

(a) Holy Island, near the Isle of Arran in the West of Scotland, is a natural haven of peace that has a long spiritual history. This very special place of rare flora and fauna came under the stewardship of the Samye Ling Tibetan Centre in 1992. The Holy Island Project aims to cultivate a harmonious co-existence between mankind and nature – a place of peace and reflection for people of all faiths. An extensive tree-planting scheme has been undertaken and the land is being managed on firm ecological principles. A Centre for Peace, Reconciliation and Retreat is going to be built and the monastery retreat centre for 108 people committed to long retreats will exemplify good environmental design with ecological strategies for energy, food, water and waste management.

(b) In northern Thailand, villagers have been helped to irrigate their arid lowlands and re-forest highlands which have been damaged by illegal logging and development projects set up to wipe out the opium trade. Water reservoirs have been developed and rice banks established in villages, providing rice on easy financial terms when the harvest is poor. There is still a great deal of work to do but this project is an example of a lead from the monastic community resulting in co-operation, grassroots initiatives and labour, assisted by joint planning and management.

(c) ApTibeT (Appropriate Technology for Tibetans) is an environmental NGO (Non-Governmental Organization) founded in 1984. It works at a grassroots level with Tibetan refugees in India, saving lives and helping them to build a sustainable future for themselves through education, training and the use of appropriate technologies. The projects are designed to give the Tibetans the skills and resources to take control of their own development.

The NGO works in five broad areas: education and training; energy; the environment and agroforestry; health, water and sanitation, and low-cost building technologies.

Procedure

1. Discuss with the children the importance of practical projects aimed at improving the environment.

2. Using information obtained from the above address the children undertake some individual or group research, perhaps using some of the following as starting-points:
• What kinds of work does the organization do?
• How does this help the environment?
• Write about one or two specific projects the organization is developing.
• How does the organization raise money?

3. Towards the end of the session individuals or groups could report back on their findings.

Activity B12
Consumerism and Voluntary Simplicity

Age range
9–11 years

Time required
60 minutes

Location
Indoors

Resources
Old magazines to be cut up, scissors, glue, glue-spreaders, pencils, large sheets of paper

Objective

To explore what are essentials and what are luxuries and what our basic needs are.

Procedure

1. Provide groups of four with a selection of magazines containing plenty of advertisements. Children cut out adverts or pictures from the magazines to form two collages, one illustrating items which are luxuries, the other items which are essentials.

2. Display all the collages and ask the children to look at them to see where there are similarities or differences. A class discussion could then take place.

3. Each group could then re-form and try to agree a list of five basic needs.

Follow-up work

A great deal of follow-up work could be undertaken here. For example:

(a) A discussion on the factors that contribute to poverty, e.g. climate, sanitation, conflict and corruption.

(b) Could we live on less? Children could investigate or discuss how the growth of consumerism has had a direct effect on the environment, e.g. destruction of rainforests, sea and air pollution, desertification, growth of some illnesses, loss of local cultures and ways of working.

(c) An interesting way to conclude this work would be to talk to a monk or nun from a Buddhist monastery to examine their needs and lifestyle.

> My Religion is Simple,
> My Religion is Kindness.
>
> If you can help others it is very good,
> Yet if you cannot do this,
> At least do not harm them.
>
> H.H. The Dalai Lama

After completing some of these activities, children may be inspired to do an activity from Chapter 8: Action for a Future.

4 Christianity and the Natural World

By Neil Ruckman

WITH INTRODUCTION BY
Robert Vint

Neil Ruckman is a director of SEEDS, a Christian group of professional artists who have worked in schools and presented Inset since 1987. Initially they focused upon the use of the Arts in RE but now have widened their activities and encourage the exploration of social and ecological issues through cross-curricular projects.

> **Important**
>
> When exploring religious beliefs and practices with your class, remember:
>
> - To use non-inclusive language. That is, use phrases such as 'Christians believe that ...', 'Christianity teaches that humans should ...', 'It is important to Christians that/to ...'.
>
> - That within world faiths there are significant variations in both belief and practice. Although contributors to this book focus on widely followed teachings (unless stated otherwise), these may receive different emphasis or interpretation from different groups within that faith community.

Christian Beliefs and Values

Activities C1 and C2 (pages 39–41) are designed to help children explore and reflect on aspects of these **teachings about the world**.

Teachings about the World

Original Harmony

Christians believe that God created a world in which all creatures *naturally* live in harmony with one another, in a state of wholeness – and so reflect His perfection. God declared that His creation 'was very good' (Genesis 1:31). Humans can all participate in this harmony when they allow God to act through them – and when people do this they can become 'images of God', and tend God's creation as its 'priests'. This is seen as the original condition of humankind – as described in the story of the Garden of Eden. This belief is supported by evidence that early tribal societies did live fairly ecologically.

God in All Things

Christians believe that God is present (immanent) in everything He has made but that He is also above and beyond all things (transcendent). This means that people can meet God everywhere – prophets communed with God in the wilderness and Moses encountered Him in a burning bush ...

> *Earth's Cramm'd with Heaven,*
> *and every common Bush afire with God,*
> *but only he who Sees Takes off his Shoes.*
>
> Elizabeth Barrett Browning

35

God's Grandeur

The world is charged with the grandeur of God.
It will flame out, like shining from shook foil;
It gathers to a greatness, like the ooze of oil
Crushed. Why do men then now not reck his rod?
Generations have trod, have trod, have trod;
And all is seared with trade; bleared, smeared with toil;
And wears man's smudge and shares man's smell: the soil
Is bare now, nor can foot feel, being shod.

And for all this, nature is never spent;
There lives the dearest freshness deep down things;
And though the last lights off the black West went
Oh, morning, at the brown brink eastward, springs—
Because the Holy Ghost over the bent
World broods with warm breast and with ah! bright wings.

GERARD MANLEY HOPKINS

Paradise Lost

Christians believe that God continually wills harmony in His creation but allows humans to suffer the consequences of disrupting it. When Adam and Eve ceased to live naturally (in accord with the order of God's creation) and tried to obtain knowledge to control the world (and to become gods themselves), they ended up losing the abundant trees of the Garden of Eden, whose place was taken by fields of thorns and thistles in which humans had to labour from then on (Genesis 3). In a similar way our modern attempts to 'play God' with nature are turning much of the world to desert.

A Message of Hope

According to the Bible, despite centuries of such destruction God declared an Eternal Covenant with Noah and all living beings (Genesis 9:8–17) and constantly called people, through His prophets, to live naturally and participate in His creative work so that the natural world could be restored to harmony. He promised that if people live harmoniously and allow Him to act through them then the desert will bloom again, the whole creation will be renewed and the harmony of the Garden of Eden restored. Christians believe that because all the prophets were ignored, God himself came into the world, in the form of Jesus.

The Trinity and the Creation

Christians believe that God participates in the world in three forms:

- God the Father, who creates and sustains the world in every moment,
- God the Son, who lived in the world so that 'the creation itself will be delivered from the bondage of corruption' (Romans 8:21),
- God the Holy Spirit, who can act through all things to renew humans and the whole creation.

Spiritual Teachings

Activities C3 and C5 (pages 41–44) are designed to help children explore and reflect on aspects of these **spiritual teachings.**

Celebrating Life

Christians believe that people should celebrate life and thank God for it – they see the whole creation celebrating and giving thanks. A modern ceremony celebrating life is Harvest Festival.

A Change of Mind and Heart

Christians believe, however, that the earth cannot be restored to harmony until humans allow God to act through them again. This requires more than obedience to a set of commandments, it requires a change of mind and heart (metanoia) so that people can perceive and respond to God's will. The need to regain this spiritual perception is a theme found throughout the New Testament. To allow this to happen Christian monks, for example, would go into the wilderness to practise contemplative prayer.

Discovering God through His Creation

Christians believe that God is reflected and revealed (theophany) in everything He has made, but that people are usually blind to this. If people open their minds and their eyes, however, they can learn when they 'consider the lilies of the field' (Matthew 6:28) and can 'speak to the earth and it shall teach thee' (Job 12:8). Jesus used many parables to show what nature can teach: see, for example, Mark 4:30–32 (the mustard seed), Mark 4:3–8 (the grain of wheat), Matthew 6:26 (the birds of the air), Matthew 24:32 (the fig-tree), John 15:1–2 (the vine and the branches).

Moral Teachings

Activities C4, C6, C7 and C8 (pages 42–48) are designed to help children explore and reflect on aspects of these **moral teachings**.

Two Commandments

Christians believe that through contemplation and a change of mind and heart people can come to love God the Creator and to love all other creatures. These are the two principal moral commandments in the New Testament.

Reverence for Life

These commandments have been expressed in the form of an ethic of 'Reverence for Life'. This term was coined by the Nobel Prize winner Dr Albert Schweitzer, but his attitude was clearly shared by St Francis and many of the Celtic saints and desert fathers. It is a moral stance well expressed in St Francis' 'Canticle of All Creatures' (see page 38).

Caring for God's World

The Bible teaches that the world does not belong to humans but to God – 'the earth is the Lord's' – and that humans are here to 'tend and keep' it – to conserve it – on behalf of all creatures. It is also taught that we do not have enough knowledge and wisdom to do this ourselves, but need to perceive God's will and to allow Him to act through us.

Living Simply

Christians are taught to live simply and reject the pursuit of wealth (1 Timothy 6:10) – a cause of most of our ecological destruction – and to share all things in common.

Visions of the Future

Activities C9 and C10 (pages 48–50) are designed to help children explore and reflect on aspects of these **visions of the future**.

The long-term vision of the future towards which Christians should work is a world renewed and restored to harmony. This is often described as a restoration of the abundance of the Garden of Eden, in which 'instead of the thorn shall come up the cypress tree' (Isaiah 55:13) and in which 'the leopard shall lie down with the young goat' (Isaiah 11:6).

A more immediate vision is offered by Christian monasteries and nunneries, which attempt to be ideal and self-reliant communities in which the monks and nuns live simple lives celebrating God and living in harmony with nature and with one another. St Francis established the Franciscan order of Friars (a monastic order), which also has these ideals. In addition to monks, nuns and friars there are many less formal or 'lay' Christian communities who try to live this way, such as those at Iona in Scotland, Taizé in France and the Northumbrian Community in England.

The Canticle of Brother Sun

Most High, all-powerful, good Lord,
Yours are the praises, the glory, the honour, and all blessing.
To You alone, Most High, do they belong,
and no man is worthy to mention Your name.
Praised be You, my Lord, with all your creatures,
especially Sir Brother Sun,
Who is the day and through whom You gave us light.
And he is beautiful and radiant with great splendour;
and bears a likeness of You, Most High One.
Praised be You, my Lord, through Sister Moon and the stars,
in heaven You formed them clear and precious and beautiful.
Praised be You, my Lord, through Brother Wind,
and through the air, cloudy and serene, and every kind of weather
through which You give sustenance to Your creatures.
Praised be You, my Lord, through Sister Water,
which is very useful and humble and precious and chaste.
Praised be You, my Lord, through Brother Fire,
through whom You light the night
and he is beautiful and playful and robust and strong.
Praised be You, my Lord, through our Sister Mother Earth,
who sustains and governs us,
and who produces varied fruits with coloured flowers and herbs.
Praised be You, my Lord, through those who give pardon for Your love
and bear infirmity and tribulation.
Blessed are those who endure in peace
for by You, Most High, they shall be crowned.
Praised be You, my Lord, through our Sister Bodily Death,
from whom no living man can escape.
Woe to those who die in mortal sin.
Blessed are those whom death will find in Your most holy will,
for the second death shall do them no harm.
Praise and bless my Lord and give Him thanks
and serve Him with great humility.

Christianity Activities

Activities J1 and J2 (pages 93–96]) in the Judaism section explore the biblical creation story and may be used to study parallel concepts in Christianity. Activities J3 and J4 (pages 96–97) could be adapted for work on Christianity.

Several activities included in chapters on other faiths could also be adapted for use in units of work on Christianity. These are asterisked in the Index of Activities on pages 112–113.

A range of introductory activities designed to help children respond to and reflect on the natural world appear in Chapter 2 (pages 15–23).

Activity C1
The Christian Creation Story

Age range
5–8 years

Time required
120–150 minutes
(Steps 6–7 can be done in a second session)

Location
Indoors

Resources
Retelling for children of Genesis 1:1–2:4 (e.g. Children's Illustrated Bible, pages 18–19, by Selina Hastings, Dorling Kindersley, ISBN 0 7513 5113 X), pictures of animals, classroom musical instruments, paints, several large sheets of paper

Objective

To improve children's knowledge of the biblical creation story.

Procedure

1. Ask the class for ideas or stories about how the world was created.

2. Tell the class that today they are going to look at the Christian creation story. Read the story to them.

3. Go through the days of creation. Ask the class what colour might be used to represent each day (e.g. blue for the day on which sky was created) and discuss what sounds and smells there might have been on that day. Write on the board what was created on each day and record the colours, sounds and smells suggested.

4. Divide the class into seven groups and give each group one day of creation to work on.

5. Each group agrees what colours they will use for their day. They then draw/paint a group picture – abstract or realistic. If relevant they can stick on pictures of animals. They can also write what smells there would have been on this day.

6. Display all the pictures. As a class, look at the pictures in turn and agree sounds for each day.

7. Create these sounds as a class or in groups using musical instruments and/or voices.

Extension activities

Children could present their pictures with sounds in assembly.

Children could use Encarta or an encyclopedia to find out about the animals in the pictures. They could research where these animals live, what they eat, how they are used by people and whether they are threatened with extinction.

Activity C2
The Bread and Wine

Age range
9–11 years

Time required
60–90 minutes

Location
Indoors

Resources
Retelling of the story of the Last Supper (e.g. *Children's Illustrated Bible*, pages 264–265, by Selina Hastings, Dorling Kindersley, ISBN 0 7513 5113 X), descriptions of bread- and wine-making processes, bread and wine (optional)

Objective

To explore how the belief that God created the world is represented in the Eucharist through the bread and wine. To consider how humankind has abused these symbols.

Introduction

This activity explores the use of the natural symbols of bread and wine by Jesus at the Last Supper and by Christians at the Eucharist. It would therefore be most effective if incorporated into a unit of work covering other important concepts and practices associated with the events of Holy Week and Easter, such as the following:

• Christians believe that Jesus died on the Cross to atone (make up) for the wrong that people do to each other and the world around them. The bread and wine, representing Jesus' body and blood, are symbols of the sacrifice Jesus made on behalf of humankind. Jews at that time similarly provided sacrifices to make up for the things they had done wrong.

• Christians believe that, three days after his death, Jesus came back to life and appeared to his disciples, giving them instructions about spreading his teachings. He then ascended to heaven. Christians celebrate Jesus' resurrection during worship each Sunday (not just at Easter).

• Christians believe that because Jesus died to save people from sin, God will forgive anyone who is truly sorry for their wrongdoing. At the Eucharist, Christians say sorry to God and in many churches say 'Peace be with you' to each other before sharing the bread and wine.

Preparation

Ensure that the children have an adequate knowledge of the context of the Last Supper to begin to understand the importance of the symbols of bread and wine. They should at least know in outline the stories of Jesus' death and resurrection.

Procedure

1. Read the story of the Last Supper to the class.

2. Explain that what Jesus did with the bread and wine is remembered by Christians and that they share bread and wine at church during the Eucharist (or Mass or Holy Communion or Lord's Supper).

3. Explore with the class why Jesus used bread and wine. Point out that these were everyday, basic foods made from natural ingredients. Link this with the belief that God created the natural world which provides us with food and drink.

4. In groups of about four, the children research how either bread or wine is made today and represent this as a pictorial flow chart starting with the plant and ending with the believer's mouth. Since most families are no longer as closely involved in the making of bread and wine as were people in Jesus' day, this research is an important stage in helping children understand how these symbols connect believers to the natural world.

5. Discuss with the class where pollution could enter the flow charts.

6. In groups, the children indicate on their charts what type of pollution might arise, e.g. pesticides, preservatives, food additives, packaging, fumes from lorries.

7. Individually, children could reflect on how people abuse the natural resources of the world and how we could stop polluting.

Activity C3
Using Your Senses

Age range
5–11 years

Time required
60 minutes

Location
Indoors or outdoors

Resources
None

Objective

To consider and discuss what makes a place special. To help children to appreciate their environment.

Procedure

1. Sit the children in a comfortable position. Ask them to close their eyes and breathe deeply and regularly. (It is better if they close their eyes, but they can sit with their eyes open, in which case they should all be well spaced from their neighbours.)

2. Ask the children to imagine they are breathing in bright, clear air and breathing out the smoke of all their other thoughts/worries.

3. Next tell them to recall a happy memory and encourage them to build up a picture of it using their senses. First, ask them to imagine themselves in the middle of this scene and to take a good look around, including behind them. Then work through the other senses asking them to think about what they can hear, touch and smell/taste.

4. Ask the children to leave their memory and, when they are ready, to open their eyes.

5. In pairs, the children then tell each other as much as they want to about their memory, remembering to say something for each of the senses if they wish.

6. Ask volunteers to tell the whole class about their memories. Focus on the environments involved and draw out what made these places special.

7. The children now focus on their immediate environment. Ask them to take a good look around then close their eyes and use their other senses as in Step 3 above.

8. Tell the children to open their eyes and ask what they could sense. What do they dislike about their immediate environment?

9. In groups, the children agree what they could do about the aspects of their environment they don't like, e.g. graffiti, and draw up a 'contract', e.g. 'I don't like the swear words on this table, so I will not write any on the table myself.'

Extension activity

The class could lead an assembly to encourage other pupils to use their senses. The style of presentation can be as adventurous as the school will allow (using videos, music, for example). Groups representing one of the senses could in turn talk about good things from their memories, followed by the good and bad things they saw in the classroom (video or music could be used as examples for any of these). Lastly each group could state at least one thing they have contracted to do. (cont. overleaf)

The style of this presentation could be as a well-rehearsed, fast, snappy poem, so that it is fun and lively. At the end of the presentation, the pupils in the audience could be challenged by each group to use their senses to perceive the world around them, e.g. 'Open your eyes and see the fiery winter sunset.'

Activity C4
Changing Our Lifestyles

Age range
9–11 years

Time required
60 minutes

Location
Indoors

Resources
Pencils, paper

Objective

To help children to think about what effect they have on the world around them. To enable children to decide what they could change to alleviate any negative effects they may have on the environment.

Procedure

1. Ask each child to write a timeline of a typical day, indicating what they do each hour.

2. Ask them to think about what they use during these activities, e.g. do they use transport or do they buy sweets? They then write a new timeline indicating for each hour what resources they use during a typical day.

3. Next ask the children to underline the resources that would cause pollution (or waste), e.g. petrol from cars, chemicals from packaging.

4. Finally, the children discuss in groups which of these pollutant resources they could do without, e.g. could they walk to school on some days? Encourage each pupil to choose at least one change they could make to their lifestyle to reduce pollution. Volunteers might be prepared to report back to the rest of the class on their progress at a later date.

Extension activity

Children could be asked to lead other classes or groups through the same analysis. This might lead to some changes on a school-wide level.

Activity C5
Writing Poems and Psalms

Age range
9–11 years

Time required
60–90 minutes

Location
Garden, park or rural location for Steps 1–2. The activity may then be continued indoors.

Objective

To explore how psalms used in Christian worship express belief in God as Creator.

Resources

One copy of Psalm 148 (see page 43) per child, pencils, paper

Procedure

1. Take the children outdoors and ask them to think about what they can see, hear, smell and touch. (It may help to do Activity C3 as preparation for this.)

2. Individually, the children now write down what they can see, hear, smell, touch as noun/adjective pairs, e.g. warm earth, cool wind.

3. In pairs, the children pool their noun/adjective pairs and arrange them as lines of a 'poem'. Once they have decided on the order, they can link the lines with extra words as necessary and if they wish divide their writing into verses, with each verse covering a different subject area, e.g. one on touch, one on smell, etc. (cont. overleaf)

Psalm 148

Praise the Lord
Praise the Lord from the heavens,
   praise him in the heights above.
Praise him, all his angels
   praise him, all his heavenly hosts.
Praise him, sun and moon,
   praise him, all you shining stars.
Praise him, you highest heavens
   and you waters above the skies.
Let them praise the name of the Lord,
   for he commanded and they were created.
He set them in place for ever and ever;
   he gave a decree that will never pass away.

Praise the Lord from the earth,
   you great sea creatures and all ocean depths,
lightning and hail, snow and clouds,
   stormy winds that do his bidding,
you mountains and all hills,
   fruit trees and all cedars,
wild animals and all cattle,
   small creatures and flying birds,
kings of the earth and all nations,
   you princes and all rulers on earth,
young men and maidens,
   old men and children.

Let them praise the name of the Lord,
   for his name alone is exalted;
   his splendour is above the earth and the heavens.
He has raised up for his people a horn,
   the praise of all his saints,
   of Israel, the people close to his heart.

Praise the Lord.

4. Explain to the class that Christians believe that the world was created by God and observing the world helps them to celebrate God. The Psalms are songs in the Bible written many centuries ago that are still used in churches today. Many Psalms celebrate the environment.

5. Read Psalm 148 to the class. Distribute the copies and discuss with the children which phrases tell nature to praise God.

6. If appropriate, the children can insert these or similar phrases into their own poems to turn them into psalms.

Activity C6
Creating Pleasant Places

Age range
5–11 years

Time required
1–2 hours

Location
Indoors or outdoors

Resources
Objects to stimulate the senses, e.g. leaves, fir-cones, flowers, smooth stones, fruit for smell, cushions for touch, recorded music

Objective

To consider what environmental factors make places pleasant to other people. To develop children's ability to think of others and their environment.

Preparation

This activity should be preceded by Activity C3.

Procedure

1. In groups, the children agree some things that create a good environment, drawing on their memories from Activity C3 and including at least one good thing for each of the senses sight, hearing, smell and touch.

2. Allocate groups different parts of the classroom or school if possible. Ensure each group has a selection of objects to stimulate the senses, including natural objects such as leaves, fir-cones or flowers, and ask them to create as pleasant an environment as possible in their area. The groups could also go into the school grounds to collect their own objects.

3. Groups visit each other's pleasant places and spend some time in them **without changing anything!** Encourage the children to think about what other groups have done to improve their areas and say what they like about the different places they visit. This could lead to a piece of writing in which children describe what the environment of their ideal place would be like.

Activity C7
St Francis

Age range
9–11 years

Time required
60–90 minutes

Location
Indoors

Objective

To explore St Francis' concern for outcasts as well as for animals as part of God's creation. To challenge children to think about outcasts and how they could improve others' environments.

Resources

Episodes from the story of St Francis may be read from the book *God's Fool* (Julian Green, Hodder & Stoughton, ISBN 0 340 39077 8) or retold using the brief outlines on page 45, which could also be distributed for pupil reference.

Procedure

1. Ask the class if anyone has heard of St Francis and, if so, what they know about him.

2. Explain that St Francis lived in Italy in the thirteenth century. The only thing he is

St Francis the Revolutionary

St Francis lived in Italy in the thirteenth century. The only thing he is usually remembered for is being kind to animals, but there was a lot more to St Francis than that.

Francis was born into a rich merchant's family. He was well educated and lived a wild life as a young man. (*God's Fool*, pages 38–40)

Then he joined the local army, which was fighting against a nearby town. During the battles, there is no doubt he killed a few people as he was very good with the sword. But he was captured and ended up in prison. He got out of prison only when his father paid some money to his captors. (*God's Fool*, pages 45–49)

Francis had many plans for his life but he hated and had no time for people who were outcasts. He was never short of food or wine and looked down on those who were – he blamed them for their own misery.

But then it seems God spoke to him and his life changed. He became a Christian and gave up all his riches for a simpler lifestyle. (*God's Fool*, pages 59–68)

Soon after Francis came back home, having been released from prison, he encountered a man suffering from leprosy. This is a terrible skin disease which causes the sufferer to be covered in sores and sometimes lose limbs. Until modern times, leprosy was believed to be highly contagious and sufferers were forced to live on the very edge of society, away from everyone else and in poverty (this is often still the case). They were exactly the people Francis had always looked down on.

But now he was different and he leapt off his horse to greet the leprosy sufferer with a kiss of peace, overcoming any fear or disgust he might feel. As the man returned his greeting, an immense joy swept over Francis and he gained a new understanding of the value of each human being.

From then on, he took the side of the outcasts, fighting for their rights and trying to improve their living conditions and their environment. He now understood the need to care for those who are our neighbours and for their living conditions. (*God's Fool*, pages 72–74)

Much later in his life Francis tamed a wolf which had been terrorizing the town of Gubbio, attacking and eating the inhabitants. He helped the people of Gubbio to realize that if they left food for the wolf it would stop attacking them. When they did this the wolf became tame. In the end it was so liked that when it died it was buried in the church graveyard – its grave was rediscovered last century. The people of Gubbio learnt that in respecting and giving to nature, they too would receive from it. (*God's Fool*, pages 218–220)

usually remembered for is being kind to animals, but there was a lot more to St Francis than that.

3. Tell or read to the class the story of Francis' early life up to his imprisonment (*God's Fool*, pages 38–49).

4. Discuss as a class or in small groups the plans Francis may have had for his life. Ask the children to write down their own ambitions for the future.

5. Ask volunteers to tell the class some of their ambitions. Tell the children that Francis had many plans for his life but he hated and had no time for people who were outcasts. He was never short of food or wine and looked down on those who were – he blamed them for their own misery. But then his life changed.

6. Tell or read the story of Francis' conversion to Christianity and his encounter with the man with leprosy.

7. Discuss who are the outcasts in the world today, e.g. the homeless. What problems do modern outcasts face? What can people do to help them and improve their living conditions?

8. Ask the children to reread and think about their list of ambitions. Have they considered outcasts and what they could do for them in their plans for the future? Give the children time to reflect on this and amend their list if they wish.

9. Discuss what the children or school could do to improve the environment or living conditions for people in need locally. Where possible, help the children to put some of their ideas into practice.

Extension activity

Tell or read to the class the story of St Francis and the wolf of Gubbio (*God's Fool*, pages 218–220). Discuss how we can treat the environment with more respect. Children could draw up a list of five do's, e.g. 'Recycle your rubbish', and five don'ts, e.g. 'Don't drop your litter'.

Activity C8
Holidays and the Environment

Age range
9–11 years

Time required
60–90 minutes

Location
Indoors

Resources
Holiday brochures from exotic locations, Encarta or children's encyclopedia, copies of page 47 for each group, pencils, paper

Objective

To help children to think about the effect of leisure activities on others.

Procedure

1. In groups, children look through the holiday brochures and decide where they would most like to go and why. They then discuss what they would do on their chosen holiday.

2. As a class, discuss what resources these activities would need to support them, e.g. cars to travel around the country, hotel buildings to stay in. Then consider what changes the use of these resources might cause in the areas visited, e.g. increased pollution from cars, trees being cut down for hotels.

3. In groups, the children find out about the country they have chosen and prepare a 2–4 minute radio report on its economy and environment. Areas to think about are how rich is it compared to other countries, what are its major industries, what environmental problems is it currently suffering from, how has the holiday industry affected this country? (Encarta will provide the answers to these questions for most

Holiday Facts and Thoughts

1. By the year 2000, tourism will be the biggest industry in the world with over 650 million travellers each year.

What about all the rubbish travellers produce? Whose country do you think it will be left in?

2. Eighty per cent of international travellers come from just twenty countries – mostly European countries, the USA or Australia. (There are over 140 countries in the world.)

Why do most of the travellers come from these countries? Why do people from other countries not go on holiday abroad?

3. Resorts in the poorest countries now make up one quarter of the world's tourist destinations but the money tourists spend there very often does not benefit that country. For example, two-thirds of the money spent in Thailand goes to businesses owned by foreigners (such as McDonalds). So the money doesn't help Thailand.

How do you think it feels when someone a lot richer than you comes to visit your country but doesn't give you anything?

4. There are over 850 lodges for walkers from foreign countries in Annapurna, Nepal. To build a lodge, one hectare of forest has to be cut down.

Which do you think is more important – the forest or the lodges? Why?

countries.) For thoughts on the last question, children could refer to the 'Holiday Facts and Thoughts' sheet on page 47.

4. The groups present their radio reports to the class.

Extension activity

In groups, children could decide on questions to which they would like to find the answers if they visited their chosen country, and suggest how they would try to do this research.

Activity C9
Seeds and Flowers

Age range
5–8 years

Time required
About 60 minutes for Steps 1–3 and 20–30 minutes for Step 5. The middle part of the activity will continue through the summer term.

Location
Indoors and outdoors, depending on where the flowers are grown

Resources
Nasturtium seeds (3–4 per child), pictures of nasturtiums in flower (or real nasturtiums), one record sheet (see page 49) and one 10–15 cm pot with compost per child, pencils, retelling for children of Genesis 1:1–2:4 (e.g. *Children's Illustrated Bible*, pages 18–19, by Selina Hastings, Dorling Kindersley, ISBN 0 7513 5113 X)

Objective

To help children understand that creation goes through a continuing cycle of change and renewal. To develop understanding of the biblical creation story.

It is best to use organic seeds for this activity. These may be obtained from the Henry Doubleday Research Association, Ryton Organic Gardens, Ryton-on-Dunsmore, Coventry, West Midlands CV8 3LG. Tel. 01203 303517. Other seeds may have been treated with chemicals so you should ensure that children don't put them in their mouths or swallow them.

Procedure

1. Give each child a nasturtium seed to look at and discuss what they think it is. When they realize that it is a seed they can try to guess what plant might come from it.

2. Distribute pictures of nasturtiums, or real nasturtiums if possible, and explain that this is what the seeds produce. Ask the children to identify which part of the plants the seeds come from. Then discuss with the class what processes bring about this change in the seeds, e.g. warmth, sun, water, nutrients from the soil.

3. Give each child 3–4 seeds, a record sheet, pot and compost. The children follow the instructions on the sheet (with help from an adult if necessary), keeping a record of plant growth, when flowers appear, etc.

4. In the middle of July, the children can collect the seeds from the flower heads, ready for growing by another class the following year.

5. When the seeds are collected, read or remind the class of the biblical creation story, noting particularly that on the seventh day God rested, having finished creating the world. In the same way, plants rest once they have finished their cycle of growth, after they have produced seeds for new plants next year. Alternatively, the story of Noah could be read as it is a symbol of the cycle of death and new life. The floods destroy the land, the Ark with the animals and people is a seed and when the waters subside the land is ready to be 'planted' with the animals and people.

Extension activity

The class could continue to observe the nasturtiums (preferably planted in a flowerbed) to see how they decay and add nutrients to the soil.

48

Nasturtiums Record Sheet

1. Seeds

Measure and count your seeds. What do they feel like? What colour are they? Record your results in the table:

Number of seeds	Size of seeds	Hard or soft?	Colour

2. Planting

Plant your seeds in a pot of compost at a depth of about 1 cm and 8 cm apart. Water the pot. Make sure you keep the compost moist as the seedlings come up and the plants grow. Put the pot in a sunny place – a windowsill, for example.

3. Seedlings

Check your pot each day to see whether the seedlings have appeared. It will probably take at least four days before anything happens. Over the next few weeks, record in the table how many seedlings there are and how they grow:

End of week	Number of seedlings	Height of tallest
Week 1		
Week 2		
Week 3		
Week 4		

4. Flowers

Check your plants to see when the flowers first come out and record in the table what colours they are:

End of week	Number of flowers	Colours
Week 5		
Week 6		
Week 7		
Week 8		

At the end of Week 8, you should be able to see some seeds in the flowers. You could collect these to plant nasturtiums next year. Count the number of seeds you could collect and compare this with the number of plants you have grown. Have you got more seeds than plants? Record your results in the table:

Number of plants	Number of seeds

Activity C10
Changing Our Environment

Age range
9–11 years

Time required
About 2 hours plus time spent gathering answers to the questionnaire

Location
Indoors and outdoors around the school

Resources
Pencils, paper

Objective

To enable children to consider how to improve their environment and to take responsibility for these actions.

Procedure

1. Discuss as a class what is good and bad about the school environment.

2. In groups of about four, the children next agree on three priorities for improving the school environment.

3. Each group feeds back its ideas to the rest of the class and a class 'top ten' of priorities for improvement is agreed. From this list a questionnaire is constructed asking each respondent to indicate how far they agree or not with the suggested improvements that the class has highlighted. For example, the choice of responses to a statement such as 'There should be plants at the school entrance' could be 'Strongly agree', 'Agree', 'Disagree', 'Strongly disagree'.

4. Make enough copies of the questionnaire to allow each child to ask at least five other pupils or adults at the school to answer it. Help the class decide how to organize the survey so that they don't all approach the same people, for example.

5. In their original groups, the children start collating the results of the survey by counting how many times each improvement suggested on the questionnaire was given the highest priority by their respondents, e.g. how many times each statement scored a 'Strongly agree' response.

6. Ask the groups for their results and identify which five (maximum) improvements were voted highest priority by most people overall.

7. In groups, the children discuss and agree how these changes can be brought about – particularly thinking about what they themselves can do.

8. As a class, discuss the groups' suggestions and identify action that each child can take individually, e.g. not dropping litter in the playground. Also agree proposals to put to the school council or a similar appropriate body. It is important that the children consider what changes they can effect first, however, so that they can, where possible, take responsibility for improving the environment.

After completing some of these activities, children may be inspired to do an activity from Chapter 8: Action for a Future.

⑤ Hinduism and the Natural World

BY INDRIYESHA DAS

Indriyesha Das, although born of English parents, has been practising as a brahmin (Hindu) priest since 1978 and is a devotee of Krishna. During the last seven years he has made over twelve hundred presentations to schools and colleges on Hindu beliefs, practices and lifestyles. He lives in Hertfordshire and is Deputy Director of ISKCON Educational Services.

Important

When exploring religious beliefs and practices with your class, remember:

- To use non-inclusive language. That is, use phrases such as 'Most Hindus believe that ...', 'Hinduism teaches that humans should ...', 'It is important to many Hindus that/to ...'.

- That within world faiths there are significant variations in both belief and practice. Although contributors to this book focus on widely followed teachings (unless stated otherwise), these may receive different emphasis or interpretation from different groups within that faith community. Information about Hinduism almost inevitably reflects to some extent a particular viewpoint of this richly diverse religious tradition.

Hindu Beliefs and Values

Activities H1 and H2 (pages 56–58) are designed to help children explore and reflect on aspects of these **teachings about the world**.

Teachings about the World

'Hinduism' is an umbrella term for the religions of the Indian subcontinent which honour the scriptures called the Vedas, sometimes dated at over 5000 years old. Many Hindus prefer the term 'Sanatana Dharma', which means 'eternal religion'.

There is a range of different beliefs in Hinduism. Some Hindus are 'monists' who believe that the ultimate reality is one impersonal spirit called Brahman. They say that all varieties and forms – living beings, objects of this world, or even gods – are eventually realized to be illusory. They will however worship many gods (e.g. Brahma, Vishnu, Surya, Shiva, Ganesh) and goddesses (e.g. Durga, Kali, Lakshmi) as manifestations of Brahman. Many consider Shiva the most important.

Other Hindus, sometimes called 'dualists', believe in one eternal transcendent God, usually Vishnu, who is ultimately a person and is above even Brahman. They say that this world, although temporary, is real and administered by a team of lesser deities (demigods), under the supervision of the Lord.

One very popular Hindu creation story describes how the world is created, sustained, and destroyed in eternal cycles under the care of Lord Vishnu. Lord Vishnu sustains the world and keeps it in balance. He has given the task of creation to Lord Brahma and the task of destruction to Lord Shiva.

FAITHS FOR A FUTURE

Vishnu appears in his world in various forms, of which the best known are the persons of Krishna and Rama.

Some Hindus believe that Lord Vishnu created this world to enable humans to perform religious ceremonies for his satisfaction so that we can live comfortably without anxiety and at the end of our lives attain moksha (liberation from rebirth).

The Bhagavad Gita is one of the most popular Hindu scriptures. Therein it is explained that we are not our bodies; we are the conscious person inside, the soul or atman. The atman is present in all bodies – animals, aquatic creatures, plants, etc. – and passes from one to another in successive births. The cycle of death and rebirth is called the 'wheel of Samsara'. These souls are all intrinsically equal in nature but are situated in different bodies according to the Law of Karma.

This law dictates that when a human being does good, something pleasant ('good-karma') will come to him/her in this, or a future, lifetime: when a person does a bad, harmful action, something unpleasant ('bad-karma') will similarly ensue. Upon dying, a person who is pious and kind to all creatures is reborn on a heavenly material planet and one who is average returns to earth as a human being. Those whose activities are mainly cruel and destructive lose their free will and thereby return as birds, beasts, reptiles, trees, etc. These living beings do not create karma but automatically rise through the species as they suffer for their past misdeeds (performed as a human). Hence the human form of life alone is one of responsibility. Some Hindus aspire to a better birth, others try to gain liberation or moksha.

Hindus are urged to understand both spirit (God and the soul) and matter. The eternal soul is distinct from temporary matter which is moving in cycles. All things in nature are subject to six changes: all objects are created, grow, remain for some time, produce by-products, dwindle and are destroyed.

Spiritual Teachings

Activities H3 and H4 (pages 58–62) are designed to help children explore and reflect on aspects of these **spiritual teachings.**

The motto of Hinduism is sometimes said to be 'simple living and high thinking'. By doing his/her social and religious duty (sva-dharma), a devotee simultaneously progresses spiritually and obtains material necessities without undue complication and without harming the environment.

Some Hindus use sitting postures and breathing exercises in order to make the mind peaceful; they can then concentrate on God within the heart. This meditation is best practised in areas of natural scenic beauty surrounded by water, flowers and auspicious creatures such as deer, swans, etc. It is part of the process of yoga which enables one to better understand oneself, God and the world. Shiva is often depicted meditating on a form of Vishnu.

For preliminary understanding of God, Hindus often meditate on the natural world with all its beauty and wonders as a form of God.

Festivals are a way in which the natural elements are used by Hindus as an offering to God. They involve acts of worship such as decorating the shrine and sacred images, the arati ceremony (offering of flame, etc.), havan (sacrificial fire), bhajan (devotional hymns), and japa (meditation on prayer-beads). Other features of festivals are dressing up, decorating the home, giving presents, cooking and feasting. Some of the items used in festivals might be:

- Clay pots and banana leaves (for eating off – they are disposable and bio-degradable).
- Mango leaves (for decorating the shrine, etc.).
- Flowers (for decorating and worship). Flower garlands are offered to the deities (sacred images), to pictures, to religious leaders, dignitaries, guests, and loved ones.
- Coconuts (all parts of the coconut-tree are useful).

- Minerals (e.g. kum kum, a red vermillion paste, for decorating the face).
- Henna (for the hair, for mehendi patterns on the hands and feet).
- Grains: barley, wheat, sesame, rice, etc. (for cooking and throwing on the sacrificial fire: rice is thrown at weddings, ground rice is used for rangoli patterns).
- Spices (for the sacrificial fire, for cooking, e.g. saffron, tumeric, chillies).
- Cotton, wool, flax, silk (for saris, dhoties, shawls, decorative cloth, clothes for the sacred images).
- Jewels, e.g. sapphires and pearls (for decorating the sacred images, personal decoration and to promote health and auspiciousness).
- Incense (made from bamboo, charcoal, ground tree-bark, with herbs and spices, etc., such as amber, sandalwood, saffron, to give fragrance. Used to offer to the sacred images, to enhance the atmosphere and create a pleasant mood).
- Metals: gold, silver, brass, bell-metal, etc. (for utensils, decorations, sacred images, cymbals, etc.).

Special trees and plants include mango, banana, coconut, sandalwood, banyan, neem, tulsi, bilva and kusha grass. The venerated banyan-tree, with aerial roots descending from its branches, is famous for giving shelter, the neem for its medicinal properties (the twigs make great natural toothbrushes), and the tulsi for providing leaves, flowers and beads (with a little help from craftsmen!), for worship of Krishna. The bilva-tree is associated with the worship of Shiva, sandalwood provides a fragrant cooling ointment and kusha grass is fashioned into sacramental rings and mats for meditation.

If you live in an area with a sizeable Indian community you might obtain some of these items from a shop there. Alternatively look in the resources section (page 109) for relevant addresses.

Moral Teachings

Activities H5, H6 and H7 (pages 62–66) are designed to help children explore and reflect on aspects of these **moral teachings**.

Since Hindus believe that the soul is the same in all bodies, they show respect to all living beings. People, especially parents, priests and teachers, are shown respect by behaving well, doing things for them, bowing down and offering flower garlands to them. Animals and plants can be respected by at least not harming them unnecessarily.

A central teaching of Hinduism is ahimsa, or non-violence. Hindus believe in avoiding violence towards all living creatures. The teaching of the Law of Karma is that any form of direct or indirect participation in violence will lead us to suffering, for example anyone involved in the use of animals for food – the slaughterer, the person who gives permission, the purveyor, the purchaser, the cook, and the consumer – will come to suffer in some way.

Some Hindus are therefore strict vegetarians, eating no meat, fish, or eggs. Other traditional Hindus are not strict vegetarians but honour this idea by following a vegetarian diet some of the time. They never eat beef, however.

Hindu households are advised to treat animals as their own children. At festivals everyone, high or low, human or animal, is to be fed sumptuously.

The cow is considered to be our mother because she is so affectionate, and is the economic basis of the traditional Hindu way of life. She turns grass and water into milk, which the villagers in India make into butter, cream, yogurt, cheese, ghee, buttermilk, etc. From these wonderful ingredients they make all kinds of food, especially the sweets which are so popular during festivals. Krishna, who came 5000 years ago, is famous for looking after calves and cows. He would give them flower garlands, paint their horns gold, and make handprints on their sides using minerals and dye. He would call them by name and they would come and happily lick him. Bulls represent dharma (religion) and are used for ploughing and pulling carts. Shiva has a famous bull called Nandi.

Killing plants also accrues some sinful reaction although it is not so much as for killing higher animals. Because plants are living beings, if we harm them some suffering will come to us in the future. Therefore to become free from the bad-karma some devout Hindus offer their food to God. In the Bhagavad Gita, Krishna agrees to stop any reaction in such circumstances although this can be done only with plants and not animals.

Trees are respected and generally are not cut down. Tree planting and digging wells are two principal acts of charity. Water is also revered; people should not even spit into water let alone heavily pollute it. Many lakes and rivers are considered sacred.

The earth (Bhumi) is also considered by Hindus to be our mother and should therefore be respected, protected and not abused. Indian dancers even say a prayer for forgiveness before stamping on her.

Hindus are encouraged to be satisfied in life, happily accepting the necessities of life without demanding more and more. Even with regard to material wealth they are taught that it comes from God and nature in the form of cotton, jewels, minerals, fruits, ghee (clarified butter), etc.

Visions of the Future

Activities H8 and H9 (pages 66–68) are designed to help children explore and reflect on aspects of these **visions of the future.**

Many Hindus believe that each time Vishnu creates the world it starts in a harmonious natural state (like the Forests of Vrindavan when Krishna played there, for example) but then is slowly and progressively corrupted by humans until it is destroyed. However if humans truly practise Hindu principles they could help restore a 'golden age' on the earth. For many the ideal is to re-establish the conditions of the rule of Rama and Sita, when natural wealth abounded and everybody was happy and satisfied in all respects. People lived in villages set in the forest or in beautiful cities with trees, parks and gardens.

- In Vrindavan, on the River Jamuna, 130 kilometres south of New Delhi, the Vrindavan Conservation Project is flourishing, funded by the WWF (World Wildlife Fund for Nature), ARC (Alliance of Religions and Conservation) and Friends of Vrindavan (based in Leicester). Here in the Land of Krishna, thousands of trees have been planted and nurtured, successfully mainly because of the involvement of the town's thirty-five schools. The project includes setting up an environmental curriculum, appointing environment teachers, establishing nature clubs and holding tree-planting ceremonies.

- In Hertfordshire, the International Society for Krishna Consciousness is running a Cow Protection Project. This scheme, begun in 1973, not only looks after cows, but also has three teams of oxen cultivating the land, providing transport and working an ox-powered flour mill. Shyamasundar, who runs the project on its beautiful 31 hectare site, has a firm and loving policy: the calves suckle their mothers, they are never sold, and the cows are milked the natural way, by hand.

- The Chipko (tree hugging) movement, which is run by a network of village women, has been functioning in India since 1973. Begun in the Himalayan villages of Uttarkhand by Sundarlal Bahugana, a deeply religious man and follower of Mahatma Gandhi, this movement fights to save the sacred hills from deforestation.

- In 1989 alone, an organization called 'Trees for Life', planted 700 000 trees in villages across India. The founder, Balbir Mathur, appealing to people's underlying religious sense, gave the whole programme a spiritual base.

- The Shri Swami Narayan Mandir at Neasden in North London, opened in 1995, is the largest Hindu temple outside India. It was built using good environmental principles; there is no steel, it has energy-saving pumps and low-energy lights throughout. To compensate for the wood used, 2300 saplings were planted in India and England.

- Ecologists believe that meat production is very wasteful and inefficient. For every person turning vegetarian, enough extra food is released on to the world market to feed twenty starving persons. Also, many hectares of land are saved from deforestation. With the understanding that there **is** enough food to feed everybody (provided we eat and live appropriately), the Hare Krishna 'Food for Life' project was established in 1982. Operating in over sixty countries it is the largest vegetarian food relief organization in the world. In London it feeds two hundred homeless people daily.

See page 109 for addresses and telephone numbers for some of the above projects.

Hinduism Activities

Several activities included in chapters on other faiths could be adapted for use in units of work on Hinduism. These are asterisked in the Index of Activities on pages 112–113.

A range of introductory activities designed to help children respond to and reflect on the natural world appear in Chapter 2 (pages 15–23).

Activity H1
Point at Yourself

Age range
7–11 years
Can be simplified for younger children.

Time required
5–10 minutes (or longer with follow-up)

Location
Indoors or outdoors

Resources
None

Objective

To help children understand the Hindu belief that a living being is in essence not the body but the soul.

Procedure

1. Sit the children down, preferably on the floor or in chairs away from tables.

2. Stand in front of the children and announce that we are going to play a game, pointing to parts of ourselves using both hands (only one hand for younger children).

3. Ask the children to point to their left foot. Point closely to your left foot, encouraging them to follow you. After a few seconds ask them to point to their left knee. Giving them a moment for them to do this, ask them next to point to their left thigh. Then ask them to point to their right foot, then to their right elbow, etc. Point at yourself as you go along and encourage them to follow you.

4. After pointing to about ten body parts in quick succession, suddenly ask the children to point to themselves. This part can be quite comical with various gestures and puzzled facial expressions!

5. Explain that, according to Hindus, the reason we are not sure where to point is because we are not the body we are the person inside, the soul or 'atman'. You might explain also that Hindus believe the body is like a vehicle and the soul is like a driver. It is the soul (or you and me) within the body which is conscious and therefore feels, sees, tastes, etc. Since animals are conscious (try asking the pupils if their pets experience sensations and feelings), Hindus deduce that a soul is present in animal bodies. Indeed they say that there is a soul in all living beings and believe that at death the soul passes into another body, just as when a car is beyond repair we obtain another. This is called reincarnation.

*If some children point to their heart in Step 4, you could encourage them by telling them that the Hindu scriptures say the soul is situated in the area of the heart (not **in** the heart).*

Activity H2
Cycles and Changes

Age range
5–11 years

Time required
30–40 minutes

Location
Indoors

Resources
One copy per child
of the activity sheet
on page 59
enlarged to A3 if
possible, pencils,
felt-tips or crayons,
paper

Objective

To demonstrate the cyclical and temporary nature of this world.

Preparation

1. Write on the board objects to study. You might list them under different headings, e.g. 'Living', 'Non-living' or 'Man-made' (the man-made category could be subdivided into mass-produced/crafted or green/non-green items). Include machines (bicycle, car, nuclear reactor, etc.) and animals (cow, sheep, etc.), a plant, a fruit, a house, ... anything! You might want to include things related to Hinduism (e.g. elephant, temple) and to environmental issues (e.g. whale, power-station). Let the children help.

2. You could prepare pupils for the activity by discussing cyclical changes in nature (as shown in the diagram below) and in their own lives (e.g. rotas, timetables, weeks, months, years). You could link this with science and practical classroom demonstrations, e.g. seasons, the growth of plants, decay under different conditions.

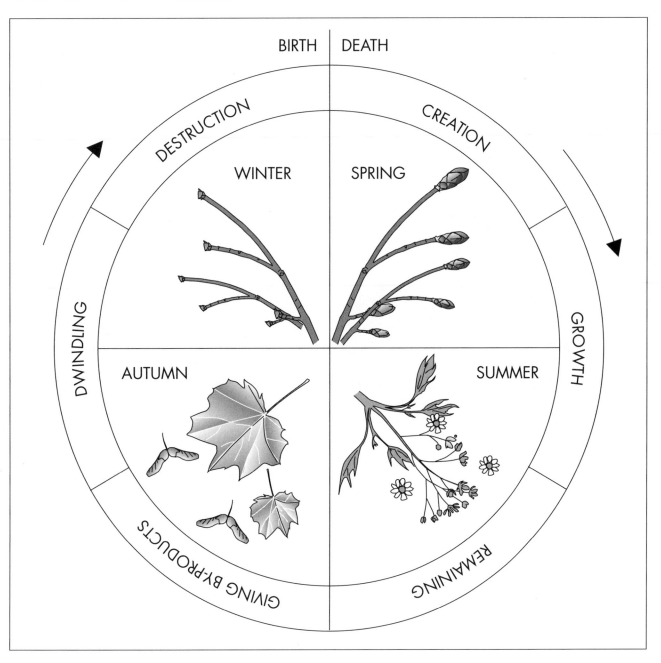

Procedure: Older pupils

1. Give each child one activity sheet.

2. Ask them to choose an object of study and write its name in the middle of the diagram.

3. Then ask them to write in each of the six sections an explanation of what happens to the object, drawing their attention to the 'Ideas to Explore' section at the bottom of the sheet. For example, for a house, under 'Birth/Creation' they could write 'A plan is made and then the foundations are laid'. Under 'Growth', 'It's built with bricks following the plan. The bricks are made from clay from a pit ...'. Under 'By-products', 'Rubbish in the dustbin ...'.

4. As a class or in groups, compare and discuss results. Do all objects in this world go through cycles and changes? Discuss some of the issues in the 'Ideas to Explore' section. Make a display showing cycles and changes in life.

Procedure: Younger pupils

(a) Copy the activity sheet diagram onto the board (or use an overhead projector). Choose an object to study and follow the same procedure as for older pupils but work as a class, discussing as you proceed. Do this for several objects.

(b) Alternatively, use the same procedure as for older pupils but ask the children to draw the changing object on the activity sheet. Use simple objects such as a tree, a house, etc.

Activity H3
Stillness and Reflection

Age range
5–11 years

Time required
30–40 minutes

Location
Indoors or outdoors: in a comfortable classroom or hall with a carpet or on a lawn in a quiet area

Resources
None

Objective

To show how stillness can assist or enable reflection, especially as an aid to appreciating the natural world.

The breathing exercises below are not meditation or religious activities; they are simply a preliminary method of inducing relaxation. You could try other methods of relaxation although this one does have a definite cultural flavour! You might point out that in the West we urge people who are stressed or suffering great anxiety to calm down by breathing deeply.

Procedure

1. Sit the children cross-legged on the floor or ground facing you. They should sit with their backs straight, put their thumbs and first fingers together and rest their wrists on their knees. Then by half-closing their eyes they will be sitting in a 'meditation pose'.

2. Ask them to breathe slowly and quietly in ... and then out. Then again, slower, ... ask them to breathe in slowly ... hold it for a few seconds ... and gently out, emptying their lungs. Again, ask them to breathe in fully ... hold it ... and slowly breathe out. Repeat this two or three times more. (cont. overleaf)

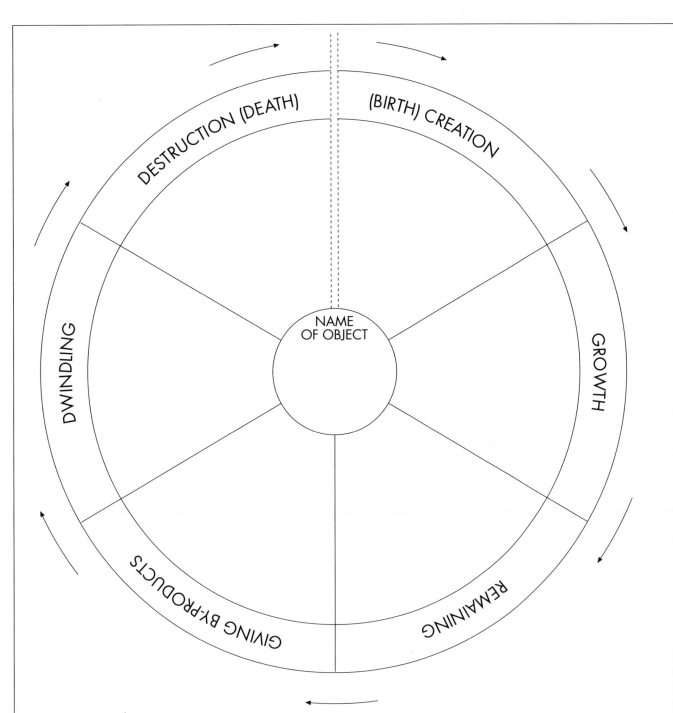

1. **Birth/Creation** Look at an object. What is it made from? Are the ingredients natural or man-made or both? Where do they come from?

2. **Growth** What does it need to keep growing? Does it need help from people to grow?

3. **Remaining** How long will it remain for? Can it last for ever? Can we help it remain longer? How?

4. **By-products** What by-products does it give? How much? Are they harmful or useful? Can we make harmful by-products harmless or even useful? Can we make useful by-products harmful?

5. **Dwindling** Do you find dwindling sad? Would you like to stop it? Can we stop it? Can we speed it up? How?

6. **Death/Destruction** What ingredients are left at the end? What can we do with these? Are they useful? Are they, or could they be, recycled? Is recycling natural?

3. Ask the children how they felt (answers usually include 'relaxed', 'calm', 'sleepy', 'happy', etc.). You might tell them this is the way some Hindus relax before thinking about (contemplating) God or Brahman. You could also discuss what types of environment help them to relax. Do they have things they do or places they go in order to feel peaceful or to be thoughtful?

4. Following this you could ask the children to listen carefully to the extract below, explaining that these are words of Krishna from the Bhagavad Gita. Speak slowly and deliberately. After each line you could ask the children to reflect upon what Hindus might understand by such a statement. Try and focus on the sense of appreciation and wonder which can arise from contemplating nature.

> *I am the taste of water.*
> *I am the light of the sun and the moon.*
> *I am the original fragrance of the Earth.*
> *I am the heat in fire.*
> *I am the life of all that lives.*
> *Of lights I am the radiant sun.*
> *Among stars I am the moon.*
> *Of bodies of water I am the ocean.*
> *Of immovable things I am the Himalayas.*
> *Of trees I am the banyan-tree.*
> *Of weapons I am the thunderbolt.*
> *Among beasts I am the lion.*
> *Of purifiers I am the wind.*
> *Of fishes I am the shark.*
> *Of flowing rivers I am the Ganges.*
> *Of seasons I am flower-bearing spring.*
> *Of secret things I am silence.*
> *Know that all opulent, beautiful and glorious creations spring from but a spark of my splendour.*

BHAGAVAD GITA, CHAPTERS 7 AND 10

Other ideas

(a) Have aids to reflection, e.g. taste some water (spring water, please!). Show a picture of a banyan-tree or the Himalayas.

(b) Make a display of pictures of the special features of nature with Krishna in the centre.

(c) Have the children make up similar statements, e.g. 'Of colourful things I am the rainbow'.

Activity H4
Festival Lamps

Age range
7–11 years

Time required
30–40 minutes
(longer if clay divas
are made as part of
the activity)

Location
Indoors

Resources
Pictures of Indian
rural life, cotton
wool, melted ghee
(use cooking oil as
a substitute if
necessary, but
not butter), plates
and trays, lighter
metal or clay divas
(Indian lampstands).
You can make and
paint your own divas
in a previous lesson
or buy them from
Indian shops or
educational suppliers
of religious artefacts
such as ISKCON
Educational Services.
Ghee can be
obtained from Indian
or specialist food
shops.

Objective

To demonstrate the simple use of natural ingredients in a festival by making ghee wicks.

Procedure

1. Remind the children of the motto 'simple living and high thinking'. You might want to explore the use of the word 'simple'. Hindus do not regard this word as meaning primitive and backward; to them it means uncomplicated and in harmony with nature. Similarly, 'high thinking' means noble in thought; thinking about life, God, and others.

2. Show pictures of rural life in India. Explain the difficulties and dangers in making and distributing electricity, involving coal mines, dams, nuclear power stations, pylons, etc. In Indian villages, before electricity was introduced, light came from lamps made of metal or clay with oil or ghee and a cotton-wool wick. Nowadays these lamps are mainly used for worship and festivals. Sometimes camphor is added for a pleasant and purifying fragrance.

3. Ask the class if candles are special to them. How do they feel in a room with candles rather than electric lights?

4. Tell the children that for the festival of Diwali, brightly painted clay lamps in many shapes and sizes are lit and put around the house and by windows. Sometimes lamps are floated down rivers on little leaf boats.

5. Children can make and paint their own clay divas at this point or in a previous lesson if you wish.

6. Sit the children around tables, each with a small pile of cotton wool. First, you show them how to make a ghee wick, once or twice, and then all make one together. This is done as follows (children could do this individually, or in pairs or threes if you are working with the whole class):

(i) Take a small piece of cotton wool and roll it tightly between your fingers so that it is the size of a large garden pea. You will have to practise taking the correct amount of cotton wool.

(ii) Take four times that amount of cotton wool and gently pull it out into a 3–4 cm square about ½ cm thick.

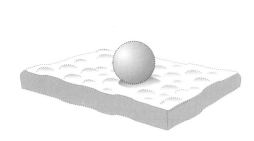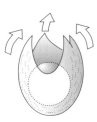

Finished untreated ghee wick

(iii) Put the square piece of cotton wool on the palm of your left hand and place the pea-sized piece onto the middle.

(iv) Wrap the square around the pea-sized piece, turning the corners upwards then twisting them together with the fingers of your right hand (or vice versa if left-handed).

Dampening the fingertips with clean water helps make a better finish for the twisted part at the top.

7. Lay all the wicks on a tray or plate and pour moderately hot melted ghee over them so they are covered. Leave to soak for a minute or two. Take out, lightly shaking off excess ghee and put on a plate to cool (or in a fridge) for 5–10 minutes.

8. When cooled, these ghee wicks can be put into divas (or on a plate) and lit to demonstrate how Hindus use them for a festival or display. The lamps will burn for 10–20 minutes (unless more ghee is added to the diva). To create the atmosphere of a Hindu festival, you might want to darken the classroom and illuminate a Hindu display or pictures and/or burn incense or play Indian music, as appropriate.

Please caution pupils not to tackle Steps 7 and 8 without supervision. The pouring of hot ghee and lighting of the divas must be done by an adult. Burning divas should be stood in a tray of damp sand, or follow your local safety guidelines for lighting candles in the classroom.

Activity H5
Cows

Age range
5–7 years

Time required
30–40 minutes

Location
Indoors

Resources
One copy of the cow activity sheet (see page 63) per child, pencils, crayons, felt-tips

Objective

To help children appreciate why Hindus value the cow so much.

Preparation

1. Revise and discuss any work you have done on Hindu attitudes to animals and cows, or introduce these ideas now (see pages 53–54).

2. Talk about pets and what they mean to us. To many Hindus the cow is similar; she's part of the family. Remind the children of the products we derive from milk. Ask them to bring in wrappers and cartons from home and make a display. You might discuss how these products are made, the tasty dishes we can prepare from them, the nutrition we derive from them, etc.

Procedure

1. Give each child an activity sheet.

2. Ask them to complete it by:

- filling in the names of dairy products derived from milk on the Indian pots in the picture;
- colouring in the picture;
- filling in the missing words.

The children could give the cow a Hindu girl's name such as Priya, Sita, Saraswati or Lakshmi. Do some research if you wish.

My name is _____ the cow. I live in __ n __ __ a.
I am wearing a flower garland given to me by K __ __ sh __ __.

I eat g __ __ __ __ s and give you __ __ l __.
The b __ __ l __ plough the land and pull __ a __ ts.

Hindus do not eat b __ e __. Some are v __ g __ t __ r __ a __.
That means they do not eat ____ a __.

Hindus say I am like their __ __ th __ __ , so they look after me
and I am very h __ pp __ !

ॐ

Activity H6
Vegetarian Menus

Age range
7–11 years

Time required
30–100 minutes

Location
Indoors

Resources
Indian vegetarian recipe books (see page 109) or menus, pencils, crayons, felt-tips, paper or card (A4 or A3 folded)

Objective

To help children understand how Hindus' moral teachings affect their diet and how milk products provide it with variety.

Preparation

1. Revise and discuss any work you have done on Hindu attitudes to animals and cows, or introduce these ideas now (see pages 53–54).

2. Talk about pets and what they mean to us. To many Hindus the cow is similar; she's part of the family. Remind the children of the products we derive from milk. Ask them to bring in wrappers and cartons from home and make a display. You might discuss how these products are made, the tasty dishes we can prepare from them, the nutrition we derive from them, etc.

3. With the children, research Indian vegetarian cooking, looking at books, studying ingredients, etc., or go to a restaurant (not for a meal!). Even if books and restaurants are not exclusively vegetarian they usually include some vegetarian dishes.

Procedure

Sit the children at tables and ask them (individually or in groups) to design and make a menu sheet or card for a vegetarian Indian restaurant or café. They should give the restaurant or café a name underlining the fact that it is vegetarian, e.g. 'The Ahimsa Restaurant' or 'Ganesh's Gourmet Vegetarian Restaurant' or 'Krishna's Café (vegetarian foods)'. The children can include on the menu sheet or card some or all of the following:

- references to the food being vegetarian, cruelty-free, kind to animals, morally acceptable (by Hindu standards) or free from bad-karma (see page 52), e.g. using catch-phrases or slogans such as:

- the restaurant's policy towards animals – in the same way that some shops state their policy towards animal testing, hunting, etc.;

- a list of ingredients and their sources, e.g. 'All our milk comes from an organic farm in Hertfordshire where the cows are milked by hand';

- the names of the proprietors, e.g. Mr & Mrs Gandhi (from Gujarat);

- small drawings of relevant subjects from India, e.g. Shiva with his bull Nandi (on the menu for the Nandi Restaurant, perhaps) or cows with Krishna;

- an endorsement or write-up from a local newspaper, temple, environmental group, etc., e.g. 'Great food. Healthy for us, healthy for animals!' (Frugal Food Magazine).

- some of the establishment's specialities.

On the menu itself, the children should include vegetable curries, rice dishes, soups, breads, savouries, chutneys, beverages and sweets (incorporating the gifts of the cow!), e.g. cauliflower curry with cheese, rice and yogurt, buttery chappatis, Indian pancakes in cream.

Extension activities

Work in groups can be expanded to form displays, each group having a corner in the classroom with posters, recipe books, pictures of the restaurant, etc. Or you could hold a competition to create the most attractive Indian vegetarian dining place.

Work done individually can be shared with the whole class.

Activity H7
Garlands

Age range
5–11 years

Time required
30–40 minutes

Location
Indoors

Resources
Large needles (preferably large darners No. 14-18), strong white thread (e.g. button thread), scissors, flowers (carnations, marigolds, hyacinths, daffodils, roses or home-made tissue-paper flowers), or you can keep the cost down by using mainly leaves, e.g. long shiny rhododendron leaves

Objective

To demonstrate how the offering of flowers displays the Hindu attitude of respect to all living beings in a festive and natural way.

We recommend the use of plastic needles (at least for younger pupils). They can be obtained from Technology Teaching Systems, Monk Road, Alfreton, Derbyshire DE55 7RL (Tel. 0800 318686).

Preparation

1. Review with the children Hindu teachings about festivals and showing respect (see pages 52–53).

2. Next you might have a discussion on flowers – different kinds, their colours and fragrances. How do they grow? When do we give flowers? What does giving them symbolize?

3. If you decide to make tissue-paper flowers for the garlands, you need to do so in advance.

Procedure

1. Arrange the children in groups of two to five at tables with needles and thread, flowers and leaves.

2. Explain that each group is going to make a garland. Tell the children to lay out the flowers and leaves in a pattern first (preferably symmetrically). Then they can carefully string them together on a thread. The strings of flowers can be from 50 cm to 100 cm in length, with about 15 cm of thread showing to go around the back of the neck. After removing the needle, the ends of the thread should be tied together to form a garland.

Many flowers can be pierced through the middle or through the sides to give different effects.

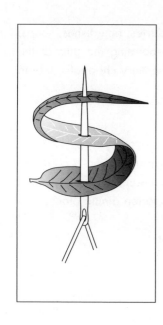

Large leaves can be strung by double-folding them in an S-shape.

3. When the children have finished the garlands, each group can show their work to the class. (Applause is always very encouraging!)

4. Ask the children to whom a Hindu might give a flower garland. Then ask them to whom they would like to give a garland.

5. Do some work in pairs. One child can garland their partner then the partner can garland them in return. Encourage the children to garland each other with respect. Tell them that Hindus generally place the garland over the head with both hands then, placing their hands together, give a small bow. The children could also say the traditional greeting 'Namaste' *(nam-as-stay)*, meaning 'Respects unto you'.

Alternatively, sit in a circle with the children and place a garland over the head of the child on your left. Then say something that you like about that child. Ask the child to do likewise with the person on their left, saying with respect some words of appreciation. Carry on around the whole circle; come back the other way if you want.

6. Ask the children how it feels to give and receive garlands. Compare and discuss feelings. Talk about showing respect, especially amongst each other.

Activity H8
Case Studies

Age range
7–11 years

Time required
40–100 minutes

Location
Indoors

Objective

To investigate some environmental projects within the Hindu community and understand how these express Hindu teachings.

Resources

Information on the projects described on pages 54 and 55 may be obtained by writing to the addresses below, enclosing an A4 SAE:

Friends of Vrindavan
10 Grafton Mews
London W1P 5LF

Cow Protection Project
c/o Bhaktivedanta Manor
Hilfield Lane
Aldenham
Herts WD2 8EZ

Mr K. Patel
Swami Narayan Mandir
105/119 Brentfield Road
Neasden
London NW10 8JP
Tel. 0181 965 2651

Hare Krishna Food for Life
c/o ISKCON Educational Services
Bhaktivedanta Manor
Hilfield Lane
Aldenham
Herts WD2 8EZ

The Young Indian Vegetarians
c/o Nitin Mehta
226 London Road
West Croydon
Surrey CR0 2TF

Procedure

1. The children can research a suitable project individually or in groups using the information provided. Find out whether they can visit it or have a speaker come to school if possible. Encourage the children to assess whether the project fits in with the main teachings of Hinduism and, if so, how. Is it based on Hindu teachings about the world? Does it express certain Hindu values? Children's findings could be presented through writing, artwork, drama, or however you prefer.

2. You might ask whether such a project will help the world. What will its effects be? Is it a practical project in which others can get involved? Do the children agree with it? Could a similar project be done at home or at school?

Activity H9
Visit to the Future

Age range
5–11 years

Time required
30–60 minutes

Location
Indoors

Resources
Pencils, paints, crayons or felt-tips, paper or card, pictures of industrial and rural India (optional)

Objective

To explore how Hindu ecological principles might be put into practice.

This activity is best done at the end of a unit of work on Hinduism and the environment.

Preparation

Review with the class the work on Hinduism and the environment you have done together. You might point out that in India 70% of the population are still employed in farming and many traditional practices are still used. However India is suffering through industrialization, with deforestation, desertification and air and water pollution increasing at an alarming rate.

Procedure

1. When Rama and Sita returned to their beautiful capital, Ayodhya, after 14 years of exile, they travelled on a fabulous flower aeroplane. Ask the children to imagine that this wonderful aeroplane arrives at school. Ask each child to imagine that they are the one chosen by the class not only to go to India, but also to travel through time fifty years into the future. They go to a village or town where the ecological principles of Hinduism have been applied with great success for many years.

2. Ask the children to make a postcard to send back to their classmates. As with most postcards, it should have a 'photo' (or 'photos') on the front with a subtitle and a message on the back. This could include a description of the place, how the writer feels there, what they've been doing, the animals they have met, etc. (and of course the weather!). They can make the 'postcard' much larger than standard postcard size if they need more room.

The postcard might describe or depict features such as temples, palaces, ornate parks and gardens, forests, clear rivers, eco-friendly people, happy contented animals, natural forms of transport, cottage industries and festival celebrations. Even Shiva or Krishna could be there!

(cont. overleaf)

Extension activity

Older pupils could imagine that the place they visit wants to produce a brochure to attract pilgrims to an ecological Hindu community. Ask the children to design and make such a brochure (e.g. using an A4 sheet folded into three). It should include writing and pictures portraying the features of the place, i.e. those suggested in Step 2, as well as the principles upon which it is based and/or the rules of the community.

After completing some of these activities, children may be inspired to do an activity from Chapter 8: Action for a Future.

⑥ Islam and the Natural World

BY RASHIDA
NOORMOHAMED-HUNZAI

Rashida Noormohamed-Hunzai has a B.A. Honours in Geography from Hull University and a Master's in Education from McGill University, Montreal. Her experience of teaching in secondary schools in Kenya and England has been greatly enhanced by her work as an Education Officer with the Birmingham Community Relations Council. She currently works for the Ismaili Muslim community in the UK in religious and cultural education.

Islamic Beliefs and Values

Activities 11, 12, 13 and 14 (pages 73–78) are designed to help children explore and reflect on aspects of these **teachings about the world**.

Important

When exploring religious beliefs and practices with your class, remember:

- To use non-inclusive language. That is, use phrases such as 'Muslims believe that ...', 'Islam teaches that humans should ...', 'It is important to Muslims that/to ...'.

- That within world faiths there are significant variations in both belief and practice. Although contributors to this book focus on widely followed teachings (unless stated otherwise), these may receive different emphasis or interpretation from different groups within that faith community.

Teachings about the World

'Islam' means 'peace' – peace between human beings, peace between human beings and the natural environment and through these, peace between human beings and God. 'Islam does not deal in dichotomies, but in all-encompassing Unity. Spirit and body are one, man and nature are one. What is more, man is answerable to God for what man has created.' (From an Address by His Highness Prince Aga Khan to the Asia Society of New York, 1979)

Islam is also known as the Religion of Nature, or Din al-Fitrah, because in many places in the holy book of Islam, the Qur'an, God invites human beings to reflect on nature in the external world and within themselves in order to understand religion (see Qur'an 51:20–21, 30:30). It is interesting to note that at least twenty-two of the one hundred and fourteen chapter headings in the Qur'an use examples from nature, such as the Bee, the Spider, the Elephant, the Sun, the Stars, the Mountain, etc.

Muslims believe that God (Allah) is One. Allah is the Maker and Sustainer of His creation. The belief in Allah's Oneness, called Tawhid, is manifest in creation through great diversity and multiplicity, which becomes a challenge for human beings, who are 'Ashraful makhluqat', the most noble of Allah's creatures, whom He has endowed with the rational faculty. Thus human beings can discover this Unity or Oneness or Tawhid through studying and reflecting on the variety and diversity in creation.

Another way of expressing the above is that Islam regards creation as a **whole** which is made up of an infinite number of parts. Thus all human beings, all animals, all plant life and the mineral kingdom are parts of one whole.

The Muslim Ummah – community of believers – is a good example of diversity within a unified whole. It consists of people of every race and ethnic group from diverse cultures and backgrounds united by a common faith.

In Islam, creation is dynamic – it is constant and perpetual: that is, it has no beginning and no end. To put this another way, creation is a circle or cyclical. Many examples in nature, such as the movement of the earth, the seasons, water cycle, etc., are cyclical and are 'ayats' or signs for people to reflect on and learn that creation is indeed constant and perpetual.

The Qur'an abounds in examples from nature, such as its many references to water. In 50:9, God says: 'We send down water as a blessing from the heavens and grow gardens with it ...'. In 30:24, the Qur'an states: 'He sends down water from the heavens and with it gives life to the earth after its death.' God also states: 'We made every living thing of water' (21:30).

The importance of water is reflected in its use for ritual purification as well as in the fountains and channels of running water in gardens which represent Paradise (Qur'an 47:15, 2:25). Both in the act of cleansing before prayers and its inclusion in Paradise gardens, water also carries the symbolic meaning of attaining inner purity through religious practice and knowledge.

Spiritual Teachings

Dhikr – remembering Allah – is vital because 'Prayer is a daily necessity – it is a direct communication of the spark (part) with the universal flame (whole).' Therefore the gist of the verse in the Qur'an 13:28 is:

Indeed the hearts of people find peace in the remembrance of God.

Dhikr may be done as a congregation or individually. It can be done as part of a large or small group in a masjid (the English equivalent is 'mosque'), which is a general place of worship. It is also done in a zawiya (Arabic) or khanaqah or jamat khanah (Persian), which are places of worship of groups within Islam, such as sufis, dervishes, etc. Individual dhikr is also done at home, in the park, when travelling on the bus, train or walking. Allah enjoins human beings to remember Him all the time:

Surely in the creation of the heavens and earth and in the changing of night and day there are signs for people who think and remember God, standing and sitting and (lying) on their sides, and who think about the creation of the heavens and the earth (and say): Our Lord, You have not created all this for nothing. Glory be to You!

QUR'AN 3:190–191

Allah is remembered by Muslims through gratitude for His mercy in providing humans with food, water, air, etc. Thus He is remembered by invoking 'Allahu Akbar' (God is great), 'Al-hamdu li'llah' (All praise is due to Allah) and 'Subhana Allah' (Glory be to God) and 'Shukran li'llah' (Thanks be to Allah) (see examples of calligraphy on page 71).

Allah is also remembered through good deeds such as caring for His creation by tending the natural world, showing kindness to animals and caring for fellow human beings. For example, growing trees is beneficial to human beings and animals and is therefore a good deed and a way of remembering God. Similarly, preventing pollution of air, water or the natural environment are all examples of caring for others.

Activities 15 and 16 (pages 79–80) are designed to help children explore and reflect on aspects of these **spiritual teachings**.

الله اكبر

Allahu Akbar
God is Great

الحمد لله

Al-hamduli'llah
All praise is due to God

سبحان الله

Subhan Allah
Glory be to God

شكراً لله

Shukran Li'llah
Thanks be to God

According to Islam the whole of creation does Dhikr – remembers Allah – in different ways:

Have you not seen how whatever is in the heavens and in the earth obeys and praises God, and the birds spreading their wings? Each knows its own way to pray and to praise; and God knows what they do.

QUR'AN 24:41

Moral Teachings

Activities I7, I8, I9, I10, I11, I12 and I13 (pages 80–89) are designed to help children explore and reflect on aspects of these **moral teachings.**

The following four concepts are crucial in terms of understanding the relationship in Islam between human beings and the natural environment:

1. God has given human beings the guardianship of His creation, because He gave us intellect and also sent Prophets to guide us. Every human being is a guardian (Khalifah) of God's creation.

2. God has given humans the natural environment as a trust (Amanat) and we will be called upon to account for our use or abuse of it.

3. Zakat – charity and goodwill towards all through sharing what Allah has given us – is a duty for all Muslims. Charity in Islam is based on the belief that human beings are all created from a single soul, therefore we must help those who need our help and share with those who have less than us. Further, charity has a much wider meaning: for instance, giving time to somebody, sharing material things, showing friendship, having good relations with others are all included. Many acts of charity in connection with the preservation of our environment, such as planting trees or building wells, are considered acts of lasting charity, i.e. they survive the benefactor and serve future generations.

4. God does not love those who squander or waste (see Qur'an 7:31).

Visions of the Future

Activity I14 (pages 88–89) is designed to help children explore and reflect on aspects of these **visions of the future.**

The name 'Islam' comes from the Arabic word *salaam*, which means 'peace'– peace with other human beings and with the natural environment to preserve balance and harmony and thus create Paradise on earth. In the Qur'an, Paradise is described as a 'garden' with running water, fountains, green foliage of many kinds, fruits and fragrant flowers and herbs.

God's creation is based on balance or justice, which is described as 'Mizan' in the Qur'an 55:1–13, the gist of which is:

In the name of God, the most merciful, the most compassionate. The merciful (God) has taught the Qur'an. He created man and taught him the explanation. The sun and the moon move according to His will and the stars and trees are obedient to Him; He raised the heaven and established balance. ... He created the earth for all His creatures. In it are fruits and palm-trees and grain and herbs. Which of the blessings of your Lord will you and you deny?

Islam Activities

Several activities included in chapters on other faiths could be adapted for use in units of work on Islam. These are asterisked in the Index of Activities on pages 112–113.

A range of introductory activities designed to help children respond to and reflect on the natural world appear in Chapter 2 (pages 15–23).

Activity 11
Everybody is a Unity Full of Diversity

Age range
5–11 years

Time required
30–40 minutes

Location
Indoors

Resources
Pencils, large sheets of paper

Objective

To enable children to understand the concept of one and many or unity and diversity.

Procedure

1. Divide the class into groups of three (or four) and give each group a sheet of paper large enough to draw the outline of one of them lying flat on it.

2. One child lies on the paper, the others draw his/her outline on it.

3. Together the group draw/write outside the outline all the physical parts of the body, seen and unseen, and draw/write inside the outline any other **positive** characteristics of that particular child, e.g. cheerful, hard-working, etc.

4. Display the finished outlines around the classroom and discuss how each human being is a wonderful example of unity which consists of many diverse features. Draw out the concept that each child whose outline has been drawn is a whole consisting of many parts, not only physical features such as organs, hair, eyes, etc., but also thoughts, feelings and personal characteristics.

Activity 12
One and Many

Age range
7–11 years
Can be adapted for younger children.

Time required
20–30 minutes

Location
Indoors

Resources
Pictures of Muslim people from different racial and ethnic groups (try holiday brochures for Muslim countries, books on pilgrimage, old magazines, calendars, postcards)

Objective

To enable children to understand that the diversity found within an individual occurs also in communities of people, such as the Muslim Ummah (see page 70).

Preparation

Prepare and photocopy a question sheet designed to help the children notice the diversity of the people in the pictures.

Procedure

1. Divide the class into groups of four or five and distribute a selection of pictures with the question sheets.

2. Draw the findings of the groups together and explain that although the Muslims in the pictures look different and live in different countries and speak different languages, they all believe in the faith of Islam, in the Unity or Oneness of God, and in the creation of God, which consists of human beings, animals, plants, trees, etc., and is full of variety and diversity. In other words, creation is a whole made up of many parts.

(cont. overleaf)

Further activities

The diversity of creation can also be explored by:

* Using videos, such as the BBC's 'The Private Lives of Plants';
* Taking the children to a local park and asking them, in groups, to identify, name, draw and colour a variety of trees, a variety of insects, a variety of flowers, etc.

Activity 13
Planet Earth and Human Bodies

Age range
7–11 years

Time required
30–45 minutes

Location
Indoors

Resources
Copy of the extract from a tenth-century Islamic text on page 75, maps of the earth, pictures showing different types of landscapes (forest, grass, rivers, lakes, etc.), possibly some anatomy charts

Objective

To develop an understanding of the great resemblance that a human body bears to the physical environment (see pages 69–70) and the idea that destroying our natural environment is akin to destroying ourselves.

Procedure

1. Display the maps, pictures, anatomy charts around the classroom.

2. Divide the children into pairs or small groups and ask them to invent (write or draw) their own body/nature similes, or do this as a class.

3. Read some or all of the extract to the class.

4. Using questions such as the following and referring to the work already done by the children, explore a range of similarities between the physical make-up of a human being and our planet earth:

* The earth consists of rocks, stones, dust, sand and minerals. What do our bodies consist of?

* The earth has mountains, oceans and rivers. Is there anything in our bodies which is like them?

* The earth is covered with grass and plants in some places. What covers some parts of our bodies?

* There are seasons in the physical world. What about a human life? Does it pass through different stages or phases (e.g. childhood, youth, adulthood and old age)?

* There is cyclical movement in the physical world such as the rising and setting of stars, the rotation and revolution of the earth, also birth and death. What about human beings?

5. Extend the comparison by discussing questions such as:

* How would we feel if somebody tried to pull the hair off our heads and bodies?

* How would we feel if our stomachs were poisoned or polluted with industrial effluents?

* How about wounds and scars, etc.?

The Body is Like the Earth

The body is like the earth, the bones like mountains, the brain like mines, the belly like the sea, the intestines like rivers, the nerves like brooks, the flesh like dust and mud. The hair on the body is like plants, the places where hair grows like fertile land and where there is no growth, like saline soil.

From its face to its feet, the body is like a populated state, its back like desolate regions, its front like the east, back like the west, right the south, left the north. Its breath is like the wind, words like thunder, sounds like thunderbolts. Its laughter is like the light of noon, its tears like rain, its sadness like the darkness of night, and its sleep is like death and its awakening is like life.

The days of its childhood are like spring, youth like summer, maturity like autumn, and old age like winter. Its motions and actions are like the motions of stars and their rotation. Its birth and presence are like the rising of the stars and its death and absence like their setting.

From *Rasa'il Ikhwan as-Safa* or the Epistles of the Brothers of Purity, a piece of classical Islamic literature of the tenth century. Scholars have held various views about the identity and political and intellectual affiliations of the individuals who made up the group of philosophers and theologians responsible for writing the Epistles, but all agree they are among the masterpieces of classical literature in Arabic. The work consists of fifty-one Epistles on a wide spectrum of subjects, such as philosophy, medicine, music, theology, cosmology and the natural sciences, including zoology and botany.

Islamic Patterns

Age range
5–11 years

Time required
20–30 minutes

Location
Indoors

Resources
One photocopy per child of the two examples of Islamic geometric patterns on pages 77 and 78

Objective

To help children to understand that Islamic beliefs about the whole and the parts in creation (i.e. the unity of God's creation and its continuity and perpetuity) are reflected in the art of Islam.

Procedure

1. Distribute the photocopies and ask the children to colour them in and as they do so to think about the patterns.

2. Encourage the children to share with the class any thoughts they had about the patterns. Point out that the patterns are made up of many parts, i.e. different shapes, which are repeated to form a whole. Also, such patterns have no beginning and no end, corresponding to the Islamic belief about creation.

3. The children can then write a poem or story based on ideas or thoughts about these examples of Islamic art.

Green, blue and purple
these stars on my paper

Seem as unending as the
stars in the sky at night

So many shapes and so
many colours
The pattern is one as far as
the eye can see

Examples of short poems based on the colouring of geometric patterns

I walk on perfect geometry
Linking shapes that have no end
I walk on eternity

Part of a long poem written by a child who visited the Ismaili Centre

Activity 15
Contemplating the Natural World

Age range
5–11 years

Time required
15–20 minutes

Location
Quiet natural outdoor location on a bright day

Resources
Quotations from the Qur'an about how everything in creation, including human beings, praises and prays to God (see pages 70–72), verse below from a poem by Sadi. A useful teacher's resource for creative visualization is *Don't Just Do Something, Sit There*, by Mary Stone, RMEP.

Objective

To help children to understand that prayer is very important in Islam and that it includes reflecting on nature, caring for it, and doing good deeds for other human beings, thus promoting peace and harmony.

Procedure

1. Do some creative-visualization exercises to get the children to relax and observe the sky and the natural environment (landscape, clouds, birds, trees, etc.) and try to feel that they are part of the environment. Emphasize feelings rather than mere observation.

2. As soon as the children relax, read some of the quotations from the Qur'an or the poem by Sadi to them.

3. After 5–10 minutes ask the children to stretch and come out of the activity.

4. Explain through interactive dialogue that just as humans are interdependent (as described in the poem by Sadi), so also nature is interconnected, thus destroying a bit of the environment can affect the whole.

5. The prayers on page 71 could be used to round off this activity.

> Adam's children are the limbs of one another
> For in creation, they are from one substance
>
> When time causes pain to one limb
> The other limbs cannot rest
>
> If you do not care for the afflictions of others
> You do not deserve to be called a human being
>
> VERSE FROM A POEM BY THE PERSIAN SUFI POET SADI

Activity 16
Contemplating the Heavens

Age range
7–11 years

Time required
20 minutes

Location
Indoors

Resources
Examples of islimi or arabesque and calligraphy (see pages 71 and 81–83) or slides of Islamic geometric art and insides of mosque domes

📷

Slides can be ordered from:

Objective

To help children to understand that prayer is very important in Islam and that it includes reflecting on nature, caring for it, and using nature to inspire art, design and architecture.

Preparation

Ask the children to observe a night sky and record their feelings about it. In cities you may need to use slides of the night sky or visit a planetarium.

Procedure

1. Show the children some slides of Islamic geometric art and the insides of mosque domes. Compare with their feelings about the night sky.

2. Ask if the children notice any similarities between the night sky and the art of Islam. Point out, if necessary, the use of natural motifs.

3. Ask the children why they think Muslim artists, architects and designers use so many motifs from nature. Explain that Muslims depict natural motifs in their art as a way of remembering and praising God and as an affirmation that humans and nature are one within the belief of Unity or Tawhid (see page 69).

The Islamic Foundation,
Markfield Dawah Centre,
Ratby Lane, Markfield,
Leicester
LE67 9RN.
Tel. 0530 244944/5.

Activity 17
Our Surroundings

Age range
5–11 years

Time required
20–30 minutes
This activity should take place within the same day for maximum impact.

Location
An unpleasant and an attractive outdoor environment for Steps 1 and 2. The activity may then be continued indoors.

Resources
None

Objective

To enable children to explore how they feel in different types of environment and thus encourage them to resist contributing to pollution.

Procedure

1. Spend 5–10 minutes in a dirty, messy, smelly environment. This can be the rubbish area of your school or it can be artificially created in a room or yard at school. Be careful to observe safety and health rules.

2. Take the children to an attractive park or garden or nearby countryside or wood.

3. Compare and contrast the children's feelings in the two different milieus. Draw out the point that human beings love beauty, peace and order and feel better and more comfortable in such contexts.

4. Discuss what can we do to prevent pollution, dirt and disorder. Is there something we can do around our own homes, streets and schools? Explore links between crime or vandalism and pride (or not) in caring for the local environment.

Activity 18
Cycles in Nature and Ourselves

Age range
7–11 years

Time required
60 minutes
(can be split into two lessons)

Location
Indoors

Resources
Reference materials, books and posters on nature and human biology

Objective

To help children to understand the Islamic belief that, since God has entrusted humans with His creation and made them guardians of it (see page 72), people must not upset the order (the cycles) in nature through their greed or ignorance.

Procedure

1. Divide the class into groups of three or four. Some groups can choose to find out about cycles within ourselves, such as breathing, blood circulation, phases of a human being's life, etc. Other groups can choose cycles in nature, e.g. seasons, day and night, water cycle, oxygen or nitrogen cycle, life-cycle of a tree from seed to a full-grown tree, life-cycle of a butterfly.

2. Ask the groups to collate their findings and show them visually as diagrams, cartoon-strips, pictures pasted together with drawings, etc. and make a class display.

3. Discuss with the class the idea that cycles in nature are mirrored by cycles in ourselves. Would we feel happy if our cycles were disturbed?

4. Use or re-use quotes, poems or prayers to reinforce the Islamic view of humans and nature (see pages 69–72, 75 and 79).

Activity 19
Stories

Age range
5–7 years

Time required
30 minutes

Location
Indoors

Objective

To use stories to reinforce teachings of Islam about the responsibility of human beings towards the rest of creation.

Resources

Stories from Islamic tradition or culture, e.g.

• *The Island of Animals*, by Johnson-Davies, Quartet Books, ISBN 0-7043-7016-6. This book is about the status of human beings and their responsibility to the animal kingdom. It is one of the volumes of the Ikhwan as-Safa encyclopedia of the tenth century (see also page 75).

• *The Birds who Flew beyond Time*, by Anne Baring and Thetis Blacker, Barefoot Books Ltd, ISBN 1-898000-00-X. This book is an adaptation of the great Sufi Farid ud-Din Attar's twelfth-century allegorical poem, which incorporates environmental concerns into the spiritual quest.

• *The Holy Man and the Magic Bowl* (see page 85) This is a short story which teaches that human beings' 'wants' are unending. Teachers could discuss with children what are the basic needs of human beings and contrast these with our 'wants' and luxuries. A class debate on what human beings need to live might be appropriate.

All these stories lend themselves to exploration through drama, mime and related activities.

The Holy Man and the Magic Bowl

Once upon a time a holy man came to the court of a great King with a beggar's bowl, and asked the King if he could fill his little bowl.

The King looked at the holy man with disdain and thought to himself: 'Why is this poor holy man asking me, a rich and powerful king, to fill his tiny little bowl.' He proudly and confidently said, 'Yes, I will fill your bowl!'

But the bowl was not an ordinary bowl – it was a magic bowl. Hundreds and thousands and millions were poured into it, but it simply would not fill up. It always remained half empty – its mouth wide open for more and yet more!

When trying to fill it made the King begin to feel poor, he said: 'O Holy Man, tell me – are you not a magician and is this not a magic bowl? It has swallowed up my treasures and yet it is still empty.'

The holy man answered quietly: 'O King, if the whole world's treasure was put into it, it would still remain empty. Do you know what this bowl is? This is the "want" of human beings.'

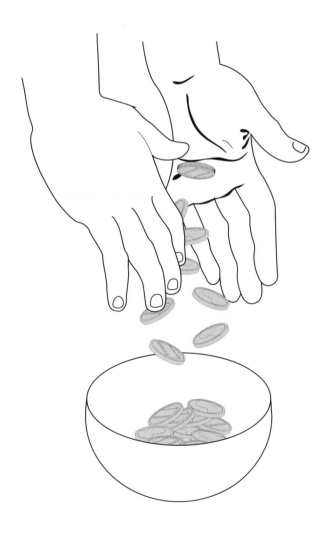

Activity 110
Planting Trees

Age range
7–11 years

Time required
40 minutes

Location
Indoors and outdoors
at planting site

Resources
Seedlings and
permission to plant in
selected areas

Objective

To enable children to plan and put into practice an act of 'lasting charity' (see page 72).

Procedure

1. Explore with the children the Islamic idea that trees are a 'lasting charity'. What is the difference between doing other charity work such as giving food and clothes to the poor and planting trees? For example, trees have longer-term effects such as preserving the environment, cleansing the air, giving shade, giving foliage, wood and fruits, providing shelter and food for many creatures, etc. Food and clothes or money is often used up fast, whereas a tree lives for many many years and keeps on benefiting human beings and other creatures for a longer span of time.

2. Explain that the class is going to have the opportunity to plant one or more trees locally. Where would be the best place to do this, e.g. around the school, at an old people's home or place of worship? Discuss possiblities and decide on one or more (practicable!) sites.

3. Plan and execute the planting with the children.

Activity 111
Only Humans Waste So Much!

Age range
7–11 years

Time required
30 minutes

Location
Indoors

Resources
Paints, etc., large
sheets of paper for
posters

Objective

To help children to become aware that humans are needlessly wasteful and to provide an opportunity to take steps to redress this.

Preparation

Collect the packaging used by the families of several children in the class for a day or a week.

Procedure

1. Divide the class into groups of four.

2. (a) Ask two children in each group to make a list of waste which humans create. What is it made of? What happens to it?

(b) Ask the other two children to make a list of the waste products of a tree which has been living for a hundred years. What is it and what happens to it?

(c) The pairs then swap lists and discuss them.

3. Through questioning and discussion help the children to understand the consequences if human beings go on producing so much waste, a lot of which is non-biodegradable.

4. Ask each group to design a poster using some of the packaging to persuade people to stop creating so much rubbish.

Activity 112
Where Did the Tigers Go?

Age range
7–11 years
Can be adapted for younger children.

Time required
60–80 minutes
(can be split into two lessons)

Location
Indoors

Resources
Map of India, two pictures showing the dramatic difference in the situation near Dahod before and after the Aga Khan Foundation's work

Project briefs and promotional material can be obtained from The Aga Khan Foundation, U.K., 3 Cromwell Gardens, London SW7 2SD.

Objective

To show children how people **can** make a difference and to provide an opportunity for them to participate in a local environmental project.

Procedure

1. Describe the project using the resources listed and the following summary:

Where Did the Tigers Go?

The overnight train from New Delhi to Bombay nears Dahod at dawn, winding its way through barren hills that show reddish soil through a thin cover of brown grass. The occasional silhouette of a dead tree is all that remains of the great forests of the Panchmahals where – as little as thirty years ago – tigers and panthers and herds of wild elephants roamed freely. And the tribal people earned a good living from the forest products and led a settled family life.

But, population pressure, poverty and overuse of the land brought disastrous results. Trees were felled without thought for the future, grass was overgrazed and led to turning a lush forest into a barren wasteland. Families were broken up because men had to migrate to towns to find work as labourers.

Two committed, caring individuals – development officers – turned the clock back by fully involving the local tribal people in restoring the forests. They convinced the people that they had to help themselves for the sake of their own and their children's future. They were helped in this good work by the Aga Khan Foundation – a private charity established by His Highness the Aga Khan, spiritual leader of the Ismaili Muslims. The Foundation's objective is to help people of all faiths who seek fresh solutions to pressing social and environmental problems. The Foundation's work is based on the Islamic beliefs and values of helping those in need to help themselves and to restore balance in nature.

2. As a class, choose a local environmental issue: for example, streets full of litter around the school.

3. Divide the class into small groups and ask them to plan a strategy to involve people in, for example, keeping the area clean or improving it. The Aga Khan Foundation uses the slogan 'Uprooting Poverty and Planting Prosperity'. Can the children make up catch phrases to suit the local campaign?

4. If possible, make some posters and carry out the campaign.

Uprooting
Poverty
and
Planting
Prosperity

Activity 113
Bird Boxes

Age range
7–11 years

Time required
40 minutes

Location
Indoors

Objective

To give children an opportunity to make bird boxes and use them in school or at home.

Resources

Picture of a bird house as part of Islamic architecture (see page 89), pencils, paper, materials for building the bird boxes designed.

Procedure

Bird boxes like the one shown on page 89 are an expression of Islamic beliefs and design. Groups of children can design their own and make them for the school or their homes.

Activity 114
Islamic Gardens

Age range
7–11 years

Time required
40 minutes

Location
Indoors, also outdoors if gardens are made

Resources
One copy per group of the sketch plan of an Islamic garden divided into four sections by four channels of water (see page 89)

Objective

To relate Islamic teachings about nature to a typical garden in Muslim culture.

Procedure

Children can design their own Islamic-style garden in groups. Where feasible, gardens can be made for the school or for an old people's home or for a local mosque or church as a long-term project.

Fountains, channels of water, water cascading over steps or different-textured surfaces, a variety of plants, trees and flowers and fragrant herbs are usually featured in Islamic gardens. There can be raised beds as well as sunken beds. Any paved areas would usually be covered with geometrically shaped flagstones, as would be the bases of fountains.

If the school undertakes creating an actual garden, the bird boxes made in Activity 113 can be used. Children can be encouraged to grow plants which encourage wild life, insects and butterflies, etc. They can be taught not to use pesticides.

To arrange a school visit to an example of an Islamic Paradise garden, write to:

The Ismaili Centre, 1–7 Cromwell Gardens, South Kensington, London SW7 2SL.

Parties of twenty children accompanied by two or three teachers would be required for a visit.

After completing some of these activities, children may be inspired to do an activity from Chapter 8: Action for a Future.

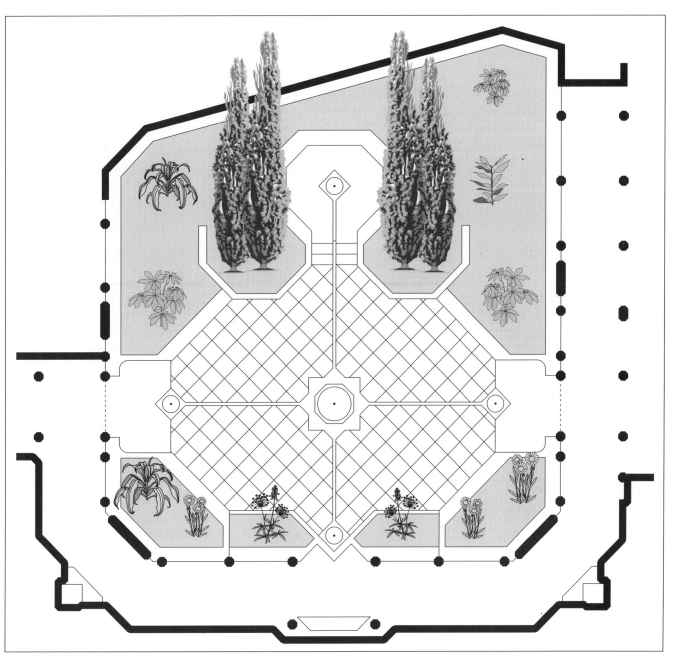

⑦ Judaism and the Natural World

BY VIVIENNE CATO

Vivienne Cato is an experienced classroom teacher and Jewish ecologist who for five years provided Inset in her capacity as Senior Research Officer at the National Foundation for Educational Research. She is Director of Education at Wimbledon Synagogue, has an M.A. in Conservation Policy and is a part-time lecturer on environmental themes. Vivienne is REEP's trainer on Judaism and was editor of *REEP News*.

Jewish Beliefs and Values

Activities J1, J2 and J3 (pages 93–96) are designed to help children explore and reflect on aspects of these **teachings about the world**.

Important

When exploring religious beliefs and practices with your class, remember:

- To use non-inclusive language. That is, use phrases such as 'Jews believe that …', 'Judaism teaches that humans should …', 'It is important to Jews that/to …'.

- That within world faiths there are significant variations in both belief and practice. Although contributors to this book focus on widely followed teachings (unless stated otherwise), these may receive different emphasis or interpretation from different groups within that faith community.

In transliterations of Hebrew words used in this book, the character h should be pronounced like the 'ch' sound in the Scottish word 'loch', and syllables underlined should be stressed.

Teachings about the World

God as Creator

Jews believe that God is the creator of the world, which belongs ultimately to Him. Humans have it on loan for their lifetimes, because ultimately 'the Earth is the Lord's and the fullness thereof' (Psalm 24). The world is God-centred rather than human-centred. As Job finds out, it is filled with awe and wonder and is beyond human comprehension (Job 38).

However, God engages people to help complete the work of creation, which is ongoing. The work of completing the world is one of partnership between ourselves and God (see Tik<u>kun</u> Ol<u>am</u>, page 92). One of Adam's first tasks in this regard was to name the animals.

Jews believe that we are to preserve the natural order of creation as God-given: mixing species and, by implication, other aspects of what we now know as biotechnology are not permitted.

Stewardship

Whilst being asked to 'Be fruitful, and multiply, and replenish the earth, and subdue it' (Genesis 1:28), the first human beings – and by extension all of us, their descendants – are created in the image of God (Genesis 1:26). Our 'dominion', it is implied, must therefore be responsible. Adam is put in the Garden 'to till and to tend it' (Genesis 2:15), not to destroy it: he acts as God's steward looking after God's estate.

The Tree of Life

The Tree of Life stands in the middle of the Garden of Eden, alongside the Tree of Knowledge of Good and Evil (which some commentators have suggested is the same tree), the fruit of which Eve was persuaded by the snake to eat. The Tree of Life has acquired many layers of mystical meaning within Judaism, being associated with the Torah (known in Hebrew as *Etz Hayim*, the Tree of Life) and by the mystical system of Kabbalah as God Himself.

Spiritual Teachings

Thanksgiving for Nature

Activities J4 and J5 (pages 96–97) are designed to help children explore and reflect on aspects of these **spiritual teachings.**

Many festivals in the Jewish year originated as harvest festivals: Pesach (Passover) in the spring, which celebrates the Exodus from Egypt; Shavuot, the festival of Moses receiving the Torah from God on Mount Sinai; and Sukkot in the autumn, marking the years the Israelites spent in the wilderness between Egypt and the Promised Land. Remembering these origins puts Jews back in touch with the early experiences of their ancestors who lived in close connection with the land. The winter festival of Tu B'Shevat – the New Year of the Trees – is another time when nature is celebrated. Humans are seen as having a crucial, mystical role in bringing about the rebirth of nature in the spring.

The Fragility of Our Existence

During the autumn harvest festival of Sukkot, Jews build temporary, leafy booths (sukkot) in their gardens in which they eat – weather permitting (i.e. not during a downpour) – as many of their meals as possible and in which they may also sleep. To remind them of the huts in which the Israelites lived in the desert after leaving slavery in Egypt, a sukkah (the singular of 'sukkot') must not be built too robustly. The roof is made of leafy branches through which occupants can see the stars and feel the rain fall. The walls are of wooden board, canvas or suchlike: not bricks. It is crucial that being in the sukkah reminds Jews of their dependence on nature and the precariousness of our earthly existence.

Moral Teachings

Tsaar Ba'alei Hayim: Concern for the Suffering of Animals

Activities J6, J7 and J8 (pages 98–102) are designed to help children explore and reflect on aspects of these **moral teachings.**

The Hebrew Bible contains many statements regarding the need for kindness to animals. The Fourth Commandment (Exodus 20:8–11) is the first statement of animal rights in history, requiring as it does that animals, like humans, do no work on the Sabbath.

In using animals to help them in their work, Jews are obliged to care for them compassionately. Animals must never be used merely for sport or pleasure, so that hunting, for example, or trapping for fur, is viewed as abhorrent. Domestic animals must be fed before Jews eat their own meal, stray animals must be taken care of and returned to their owners, and no animal may be slaughtered within sight of its parent or child.

Kashrut

Most rules of kash<u>rut</u> (the system of keeping kosher) come from the Book of Leviticus in the Hebrew Bible. Its main features are:

1. Only animals that have cloven hooves and also chew the cud, and fish that have both fins and scales are permitted for food.

2. Milk and meat must not be eaten at the same meal.

3. Food animals must be killed by a kosher method using shehita (ritual slaughter). This is intended to kill the animal as quickly and painlessly as possible.

Judaism does not require vegetarianism, although some commentators argue that the Hebrew Bible implicitly encourages it. In the Garden of Eden, for example, the diet prescribed was vegetarian only.

Nowadays some Jews are advocating widening the concept of kash<u>rut</u> to include other Jewish ethical principles on how we 'consume' food and other resources. Adding in, for example, Bal Tash<u>h</u>it (see below), Tsa<u>ar</u> Ba'a<u>lei</u> <u>H</u>ayim (see page 91) or Tik<u>kun</u> Ol<u>am</u> (see below) to traditional kash<u>rut</u> has resulted in a broader system which is being called Eco-Kash<u>rut</u>.

Bal Tashḥit: Do Not Destroy or Waste

Jewish literature from the Bible onwards advocates wise stewardship. Adam and Eve were asked by God to 'work and guard' the Garden of Eden. Humans live in the world and therefore must use its resources, but we are its guardians who must pass it on to our children in as least a good a state as we found it. The ruling of Bal Tash<u>h</u>it derives from Deuteronomy 20:19–20. The rabbis argued that if destroying trees was forbidden even in the extreme circumstances of war, then how much more so in peacetime? They extrapolated from trees to waste in all areas of human life.

Visions of the Future

Activities J9 and J10 (pages 101–104) are designed to help children explore and reflect on aspects of these **visions of the future.**

Tikkun Olam: The Healing/Repair of the World

In Judaism, the world is held to be in a state of imperfection in which it is human beings' role to bring about, in partnership with God, a betterment. This healing of the world is pursued in many ways, principally in carrying out all of God's commandments (of which there are 613 given throughout the Torah). Tik<u>kun</u> Ol<u>am</u> also has a strong element of environmental and social justice: Jews are commanded to seek justice, and this is interpreted as justice for the natural as well as the human world. The practical implications of this are brought out in many sayings and stories.

The Prophetic Vision

The Prophets, Isaiah especially, spoke frequently of the messianic future when the deserts will bloom and 'they shall not hurt nor destroy in all My holy mountain' (Isaiah 11:9). The Jewish concept of history sees time as both cyclic (the cycle of the year) and linear. Jews work to bring about the perfection of the world so as to make way for the arrival of the Messiah. A taste of this world to come exists now in the Sabbath, when work is suspended for 25 hours and Jews create an oasis in time to step out of their ordinary lives.

Judaism Activities

S everal activities included in chapters on other faiths could be adapted for use in units of work on Judaism. These are asterisked in the Index of Activities on pages 112–113.

A range of introductory activities designed to help children respond to and reflect on the natural world appear in Chapter 2 (pages 15–23).

Activity J1
Naming the Animals

Age range
5–7 years

Time required
40 minutes

Location
Indoors

Resources
Recording of animal sounds (CD available from BBC Recordings), pictures of animals, *Does God Have a Big Toe?* by Marc Gellman (HarperCollins, ISBN 0 06 440453 6)

Objective

To develop a sense of the diversity within the animal kingdom and to identify with Adam's role in naming the animals.

Preparation

Prepare a sound-effects tape of animal noises.

Procedure

1. Play the sound-effects tape and ask the children to identify the noises.

2. Tell or remind the children that in the Bible story Adam was asked to give names to the animals (Genesis 2:19–20). Using picture prompts, children in pairs devise – like Adam – descriptive names for animals of their choice.

3. Each pair presents their names to the class, who guess each animal's identity.

4. Read to the class 'Adam's Animals' from *Does God Have a Big Toe?* – an amusing midrash (rabbinic commentary) on the biblical story.

Activity J2
The Days of Creation

Age range
7–11 years

Time required
70 minutes

Location
Indoors

Resources
Copies of Genesis 1:1–2:3 (see pages 94–95), dressing-up clothes, scrap materials, percussion instruments

Objective

To explore the concept of God as the Creator of the world, and to develop a sense of the cumulative nature of creation as expressed in the biblical story.

Preparation

1. Make copies of Genesis 1:1–2:3 (see pages 94–95) – one between two is adequate.

2. Set up the room to include an open space for presenting performances.

Procedure

1. Hand out copies of Genesis 1:1–2:3 (the Seven Days of Creation) and have the children read them. Alternatively, read the story aloud to them and have them follow it.

2. Divide the class or let them form themselves into seven groups, or six if you prefer to leave out the Sabbath, in which the only 'character' is God. Allocate each group one day from the story. (cont. on page 96)

The Seven Days of Creation

In the beginning of God's creating the heavens and the earth, when the earth was formless and empty, with darkness upon the face of the deep, and the Divine Presence hovered upon the surface of the waters, God said, 'Let there be light,' and there was light. God saw that the light was good, and God separated between the light and the darkness. God called to the light: 'Day', and to the darkness He called: 'Night'. And there was evening and there was morning, **one day**.

God said, 'Let there be a firmament in the midst of the waters, and let it separate between water and water.' So God made the firmament, and separated between the waters which were beneath the firmament and the waters which were above the firmament. And it was so. God called to the firmament: 'Heaven'. And there was evening and morning, **a second day**.

God said, 'Let the waters beneath the heaven be gathered into one area, and let the dry land appear'. And it was so. God called to the dry land 'Earth', and to the gathering of waters He called 'Seas'. And God saw that it was good. God said, 'Let the earth sprout vegetation: herb yielding seeds, fruit trees yielding fruit each after its kind, containing its own seed on the earth.' And it was so. And the earth brought forth vegetation: herb yielding seed after its kind, and trees yielding fruit, each containing its seed after its kind. And God saw that it was good. And there was evening and there was morning, **a third day**.

God said, 'Let there be lights in the firmament of the heaven to separate between the day and the night; and they shall serve as signs, and for festivals, and for days and years; and they shall serve as lights in the firmament of heaven to shine upon the earth.' And it was so. And God made the two great lights, the greater light to dominate the day and the lesser light to dominate the night, and the stars. And God set them in the firmament of the heaven to give light upon the earth, to dominate by day and by night, and to separate between the light and the darkness. And God saw that it was good. And there was evening and there was morning, **a fourth day**.

God said, 'Let the waters teem with teeming living creatures, and fowl that fly about over the earth across the expanse of the heavens.' And God created the great sea-giants and every living being that creeps, with which the waters teemed after their kinds; and all winged fowl of every kind. And God saw that it was good. God blessed them, saying, 'Be fruitful and multiply, and fill the waters in the seas; but the fowl shall increase on the earth.' And there was evening and there was morning, **a fifth day**.

The Seven Days of Creation (continued)

God said, 'Let the earth bring forth living creatures, each according to its kind: cattle, and creeping things, and beasts of the land each according to its kind.' And it was so. God made the beast of the earth according to its kind, and the cattle according to its kind, and every creeping being of the ground according to its kind. And God saw that it was good.

And God said, 'Let us make Man in Our image, after Our likeness. They shall rule over the fish of the sea, the birds of the sky, and over the cattle, the whole earth, and every creeping thing that creeps upon the earth.' So God created Man in His image, in the image of God He created him; male and female created He them. God blessed them and God said to them, 'Be fruitful and multiply, fill the earth and subdue it; and rule over the fish of the sea, the bird of the sky, and every living thing that moves on the earth.'

God said, 'Behold, I have given to you all herb yielding seed that is on the surface of the entire earth, and every tree that has seed-yielding fruit; it shall be yours for food. And to every beast of the earth, to every bird of the sky, and to everything that moves on the earth, within which there is a living soul, every green herb is for food.' And it was so. And God saw all that He had made, and behold it was very good. And there was evening and there was morning, **the sixth day**.

Thus the heaven and the earth were finished, and all their array. By the seventh day God completed His work which He had done, and He abstained on the seventh day from all His work which He had done. God blessed **the seventh day** and sanctified it because on it He abstained from all His work which God created to make.

Genesis 1:1–2:3

3. The groups now have, say, 20 minutes in which to prepare a 3–5 minute presentation of their day and what was created on it. They can improvise a playlet, do a mime or dance, or sing a song: it is up to them. The clothes and materials are available to make props and costumes, the instruments for sound-effects.

4. At the end of the 20 minutes, the groups in turn present their 'day' to the rest of the class, in the order of the creation story.

5. You may wish, as a follow-up, to ask the class to discuss or respond in writing to these questions:

- Why are the various parts of the earth created in this order?
- What does it mean for us that human beings were created last of all?
- Why is a day of rest included in the story?
- Do you think that the world took just one week to make?

Activity J3
The Tree of Life

Age range
7–11 years

Time required
30 minutes

Location
Indoors and outdoors if a real tree is used

Resources
Bible(s) (at least one), pencils, scrap materials for modelling, a tree, large houseplant or branch

Objective

To understand some of the hidden meanings within the concept of the Tree of Life.

Procedure

1. Tell the story of the Garden of Eden (if not already known), focusing on the Tree of Knowledge of Good and Evil and the Tree of Life (Genesis 2:9, 16–17, 3:1–24).

2. Discuss with the class what they think the fruit on the original Tree of Knowledge of Good and Evil was. Was this tree the same as the Tree of Life? (Check the text.) Some rabbis think so. The Torah is known as *Etz Hayim,* 'The Tree of Life'.

3. What would hang from the children's Tree of Life? Ideas may include abstract ideas (e.g. love) as well as concrete ones (e.g. a picture of my baby sister, my football boots).

4. Have the children draw, write or model their 'fruit' and hang it on, preferably, a real tree. Make this a 'tree-dressing' day. You could adopt this tree for year-round observation. Otherwise use a houseplant or even a branch (found on the ground, not cut off specially for this exercise).

Activity J4
Into the Desert

Age range
5–11 years

Time required
20 minutes

Location
Indoors

Resources
Rainstick or equivalent (optional)

Objective

To 'go' on the journey of the Israelites through the desert after the Exodus from Egypt. To enable children to feel, as the Israelites may have done, that nature will protect them.

Procedure

1. Settle the children comfortably, maybe seated on a carpet.

2. Tell them they will be going on an imaginary journey back in time and to another place. Ask them to close their eyes.

3. Slowly and calmly, allowing adequate pauses for the children to experience what you are saying to them, tell the following narrative, using your own words and embellishing this outline where you see fit:

We are going to leave here and travel back in time, thousands of years ... You are walking through the desert ... Look around you, what do you see? Feel the heat, the burning sand ... You are with your family and thousands of others, walking. What are you wearing? ... It's getting later in the day and you need to find somewhere to camp for the night. Suddenly you glimpse trees: it must be an oasis! You reach it, find fresh water ... Now you need to build a shelter. Use branches to build a hut: use rugs for the walls, leafy branches for the roof ... You lie down to go to sleep in your hut. As you close your eyes you can see stars through the leafy roof ... You wake to the sound of rain pattering on the roof [rainstick] and start your day.

4. The children will need to 'debrief' from this experience by talking about how it felt for them. To make the link with Sukkot, ask them specifically about building the hut and how they felt staying in it. Did it feel secure, cosy, dangerous?

Activity J5
A Model Sukkah

Age range
5–11 years

Time required
60–90 minutes

Location
Indoors

Resources
Photographs of a real sukkah, cardboard boxes (supermarket size), scissors, glue, scrap cardboard, scrap fabric, cuttings of twigs and branches, pencils, paper

Objective

To understand the concept of the temporary booth (sukkah) in which Jewish families live during Sukkot.

Preparation

1. Prepare sets of tables to accommodate groups of three children working together on a model.

2. Lay out resources for easy access: preferably not all grouped in one spot.

Procedure

1. Show pictures of sukkot (harvest booths), preferably in the context of learning about the festival of Sukkot.

2. Explain the key requirements that a sukkah should:

- have a leafy roof through which the stars can be seen at night,
- have between two and a half and four walls,
- be decorated beautifully.

Since a family will be eating and maybe even sleeping in it for eight days, it needs to have a table and chairs and maybe beds.

3. Demonstrate how a box might be converted into a hut by using the open side as one 'wall' and cutting strips of cardboard out of the 'roof'.

4. Group the children into threes for building a model sukkah. They can use any available materials to decorate and furnish the inside of their huts. It is advisable to leave threading in the leafy roof until last.

Extension activity

In the context of gratitude for the harvest, ask the children what they are grateful for in their lives. They could each write or draw these items or concepts on paper 'leaves' which are then used to cover the outside of their huts.

Activity J6
A Talmudic Debate

Age range
9–11 years

Time required
60 minutes

Location
Indoors

Resources
Selection of enlarged quotations (see page 99), glue, large sheets of sugar paper or newsprint, marker pens or felt-tips

Objective

To consider in depth ancient Jewish teachings on Tsaar Ba'alei Hayim (concern for the suffering of animals). To enable children to respond within an authentically Jewish formula by creating their own 'talmudic' commentaries.

Introduction

The Talmud was created by the rabbis of the fifth and sixth centuries C.E in Babylonia and Israel.

It is a systematic commentary on the Mishnah (the code of Jewish law) that evolved slowly as subsequent generations of rabbis added their comments to the original discussion text. In this way the teachings of Judaism are renewed each generation, and continue to be so.

A page of Talmud is laid out in concentric layers of commentary, with the original text in the middle.

In this activity, pupils will be acting as 'rabbis' making commentaries on biblical texts, in this case extracts concerned with animal welfare.

Preparation

1. Enlarge some or all of the quotations provided on page 99 and glue each onto the middle of its own poster-size sheet. This is the beginning of a page of 'Talmud'.

2. Arrange the room so that pupils can work in groups around tables big enough to accommodate a poster.

Procedure

1. Divide the class into groups of three and allocate each group a poster.

2. Each group's initial task is to read and discuss their quotation then write their responses to it in blocks grouped around the original text. These comments should be written immediately adjacent to the text.

3. Groups next exchange posters, read their new quotation with its ring of comments, then add their own opinions: including commenting on the first ring of comments! This forms a second layer around the original text.

4. If there is time, the posters can be exchanged again.

5. Allow time at the end to display the posters so that the whole class can inspect each other's work.

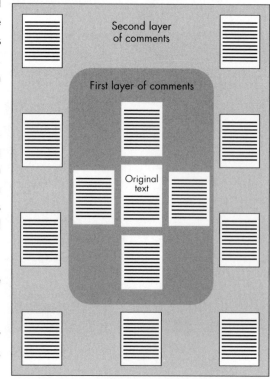

When you see the donkey of your enemy crouching under its burden and you would not help him raise it, you must nevertheless raise it with him.

EXODUS 23:5

A righteous person has regard for the life of his animals.

PROVERBS 12:10

The seventh day is a Shabbat of the Eternal your God: you shall not do any work – you, your son or your daughter, your male or female servant, your ox or your donkey or any of your cattle...

DEUTERONOMY 5:14

If an animal falls into a ditch (on the Sabbath), bring pillows and bedding and place them under it (for it cannot be removed until after the Sabbath ends).

BABYLONIAN TALMUD, SHABBAT 128B

If, on your way you happen upon a bird's nest in a tree or on the ground, with the baby birds or eggs in it, and the mother is sitting over the fledglings or on the eggs, do not take the mother with her young. Let the mother go and take only the young. This way you will fare well and have a long life.

DEUTERONOMY 22:6–7

Rabbi Judah HaNassi watched a calf being led to slaughter. The animal broke from the herd and hid itself under the rabbi's clothing, crying for mercy. But he pushed it away, saying, 'Go! For you were destined for this!' They said in heaven, 'Since he showed no compassion, let us bring suffering upon him.' For years afterwards, the rabbi suffered from a series of painful illnesses. One day his servant was sweeping the house. She was about to sweep away some young weasels she found lying on the floor. 'Leave them alone!' he said to her. Then they said of him in heaven, 'Since he has shown compassion, let us be compassionate with him', and he was cured.

BABYLONIAN TALMUD, BABA METZIA 85

Do not plough with an ox and a donkey together.

DEUTERONOMY 22:10

You shall not muzzle an ox in its threshing.

DEUTERONOMY 25:4

Activity J7
Ethical Food Choices

Age range
7–11 years

Time required
75–90 minutes

Location
Indoors

Resources
Hamburger carton, egg box, can of tuna, apple, large sheets sugar paper (optional)

Objective

To develop an understanding of personal and communal criteria for choosing what may be eaten: including an understanding of the social origins of kash<u>rut</u>.

Procedure

1. Ask the class to list all the foods and drinks they consumed the previous day.

2. As a class, group these into categories, e.g. meat, dairy, vegetables etc.

3. Say, 'It looks as if between us we eat most things. Is there anything you wouldn't eat?' Children will offer suggestions of 'disgusting' foods, e.g. snails.

4. Pass round the class prompts such as a hamburger carton, an egg box, a can of tuna, an apple to elicit suggestions of wider values for choosing foods than merely personal likes and dislikes. The prompts should bring up issues of animal welfare, endangered species, organic farming, over-packaging and so on.

5. In small groups, children next discuss their personal values in order to come up with a collective statement of principles for food choices to be presented (possibly as a large poster) to the class.

6. Referring to the difficulty with which the children probably agreed their final versions, draw an analogy with religious groups, including Jews, who have formulated rules on what is acceptable for them to eat.

You may wish to relate the ethical concerns raised by the prompts or groups to statements in the Bible, e.g. these below.

> *An ox or a sheep or a goat, you may not slaughter it and its offspring on the same day.*
>
> LEVITICUS 22:28

> *You shall not muzzle an ox whilst it is threshing (grain).*
>
> DEUTERONOMY 25:4

> *A righteous person has regard for the life of his animal.*
>
> PROVERBS 12:10

Activity J8
Waste Not

Age range
7–11 years

Time required
60 minutes

Location
Indoors

Resources
Lunch-box packed with a typical lunch including paper (a bag), plastic, aluminium (can or foil), packaged food (e.g. juice carton), unpackaged food (fruit); one copy per pair of the Bal Tashhịt quotations on page 102

Objective

To understand how much of modern life leads to wastefulness and that concerns about waste are ancient. To give children an opportunity to take steps to remedy waste in their own lives.

Procedure

1. Open the lunch-box and for **each** item ask: 'Where does this come from and where does it go after lunch is over?' Ask this question for each item of packaging. Supplement pupils' answers with environmental information.

2. Concerns about waste are not new. Discuss Deuteronomy 23:13–15 (see page 102). Is it surprising to find this in the Bible?

3. Hand out the sheets with quotations on the law of Bal Tashhịt: Do Not Waste. In pairs, pupils prepare to answer in class discussion: According to these Jewish laws about waste, what is forbidden? What is allowed?

4. Encourage pupils to identify one area of waste in their own lives that they would be prepared to remedy.

This activity appears with thanks to Shomrei Adamah.

Activity J9
Old and New

Age range
9–11 years

Time required
60 minutes

Location
Indoors

Resources
Copies of the two quotations on page 103, materials for writing, drawing or modelling

Objective

To understand that Jewish writers through history have thought about what a perfect future might be like. To allow children to add their own visions.

Procedure

1. Compare the two visions of the future written by Isaiah and Judy Chicago, both Jews (see page 103).

2. What is the children's own vision of the ideal future? Discuss as a class.

3. Either individually or in small groups, the children can draw, model or write about this future time.

Bal Tashhit: Do Not Waste

There will be an area beyond the military camp where you can relieve yourself. You will have a spade among your weapons; and after you have squatted, you will dig a hole and cover your excrement.

DEUTERONOMY 23:13–15

When you lay siege and battle against a city for a long time in order to capture it, you must not destroy its trees, wielding an axe against them. You may eat of them, but you must not cut them down. Are the trees of the field human to withdraw before you into the besieged city? Only trees which you know do not yield food may be destroyed; you may cut them down for constructing siege works against the city that is waging war on you, until it has been captured.

DEUTERONOMY 20:19–20

Whoever breaks vessels or rips up garments, destroys a building, stops up a fountain or ruins food is guilty of violating the prohibition of Bal Tashhit

BABYLONIAN TALMUD, KIDDUSHIN 32A (1ST CENTURY)

Whenever Rav Hisda had to walk among thorns and thistles, he used to lift up his garment, saying, 'If my body is scratched, it will heal itself; but if my garment is torn, it will not heal itself.'

BABYLONIAN TALMUD, BABA KAMMA 91B (1ST CENTURY)

One is permitted to cut down a barren tree even if one does not need it. So too, an old food tree that produces an amount too small to bother with may be cut down.

RABBI MOSES MAIMONIDES, MISHNEH TORAH (12TH CENTURY)

If a person kills a tree before its time, it is like having murdered a soul.

REBBE NACHMAN OF BRATSLAV (EARLY 19TH CENTURY)

When God created the first human beings, God led them around the garden of Eden and said: 'Look at my works! See how beautiful they are – how excellent! For your sake I created them all. See to it that you do not spoil and destroy My world; for if you do, there will be no-one else to repair it.'

MIDRASH ECCLESIASTES RABBAH (1ST CENTURY)

Old and New

The wolf shall also dwell with the lamb, and the leopard shall lie down with the kid; and the calf and the young lion and the fatling together; and a little child shall lead them. And the cow and the bear shall feed; their young ones shall lie down together; and the lion shall eat straw like the ox ... They shall not hurt nor destroy in all my holy mountain: for the earth shall be full of the knowledge of God, as the waters cover the sea.

ISAIAH 11:6,7,9. 8TH CENTURY B.C.E.

And then all that has divided us will merge
And then compassion will be wedded to power
And then softness will come to a world that is harsh and unkind
And then both men and women will be gentle
And then both women and men will be strong
And then no person will be subject to another's will
And then all will be rich and free and varied
And then the greed of some will give way to the needs of many
And then all will share equally in the earth's abundance
And then all will care for the sick and the weak and the old
And then all will nourish the young
And then all will cherish life's creatures
And then all will live in harmony with each other and the earth
And then everywhere will be called Eden once again.

JUDY CHICAGO MERGER: A VISION OF THE FUTURE. LATE 20TH CENTURY C.E.

Activity J10
Honi the Circle-Maker

Age range
7–11 years

Time required
60 minutes

Location
Indoors and outdoors if tree planted

Resources
Photographs of local area (optional), pencils, paper, a tree seedling (optional) and permission to plant it.

Objective

To raise awareness that everyone has a part to play in making the world a better place for future generations and bringing about Tikkun Olam (healing/repair of the world).

Procedure

1. Discuss with the children their local area, preferably with photographs. How old is it, or parts of it? Who built and/or planted it? Were they doing so for themselves or for future generations? What effect might thinking of the future have had on their choices of what to build or plant?

2. Have the children made or planted anything that will last a long time – even after their lifetimes? Is this important? (Ideas could be listed first.)

3. Introduce the story of Honi, which shows that such concerns are not new:

While the sage, Honi, was walking along a road, he saw a man planting a carob tree. Honi asked him, 'How long will it take for this tree to bear fruit?'

'Seventy years,' replied the man.

Honi then asked, 'Are you so healthy a man that you expect to live that length of time and eat its fruit?'

The man answered, 'I found a fruitful world because my ancestors planted it for me. Likewise I am planting for my children.'

BABYLONIAN TALMUD, TAANIT 23A (200–600 C.E.)

4. The children can turn the story into a mini-drama, a television interview, a song or a cartoon-strip.

5. If feasible, finish by planting something for the future, preferably a tree. Involve the children in planning what to plant and where if practicable.

After completing some of these activities, children may be inspired to do an activity from Chapter 8: Action for a Future.

⑧ Action for a Future

BY ROBERT VINT

The activities in the preceding chapters encourage children to **explore** a range of traditional religious teachings about the world and to **reflect** upon these in order to develop and articulate their own personal beliefs and values.

Moral development involves learning to act in the world in accordance with our beliefs and values, and one of the great challenges of our multicultural society is for us all to live and work with people holding diverse beliefs and values.

In this chapter we suggest some general types of practical **actions** that could follow on from study of religious teachings – but specific actions should come from the children's ideas and the outcome of classroom discussion.

experience ⟶ explore ⟶ reflect ⟶ **act**

Not Just an Academic Exercise!

Schools are not just factories for filling children's heads with information, and any school that does not relate what is being taught in the classroom to the life of the school and the life of the children is not reaching its full potential. Any member of a religion knows that their faith is not just a set of ideas but affects the way that they live each day and provides the core motivation for the activities of their community. Being 'green' likewise is not just about understanding environmental issues but about living in a way that addresses the problems.

All this is relevant because a school is a community with a common set of values. Schools have a legal responsibility to promote the spiritual and moral development of their pupils thus one of their tasks is to help children to learn to live in a way that reflects their beliefs and values.

5.1 Pupils' spiritual, moral, social and cultural development
The curriculum of a maintained school must promote the spiritual, moral, cultural, mental and physical development of pupils and of society; and prepare pupils for the opportunities, responsibilities and experiences of adult life.

OFSTED HANDBOOK, 1993, PAGE 7

Pupils should be able to move from the taught morality which is characteristic of the very young, and an essential pre-requisite of moral development, to a position where their values and judgements spring from internal sources and allow them to be mature, autonomous, decision-taking and responsible individuals.

OFSTED DISCUSSION PAPER ON SPIRITUAL, MORAL, SOCIAL AND CULTURAL DEVELOPMENT, 1994, SECTION 3.2

A school is also part of the wider world and not an ivory tower – everything we do there will directly or indirectly improve or damage the environment.

This book contains a wide range of activities aiming to encourage children to develop their own beliefs and values, without indoctrination. Some activities also suggest ways in which children could respond by expressing these values through various projects. This final chapter offers some ideas for integrating such activities into the ongoing life of the school.

Sustainability

'Sustainability' has now become the key concept in environmental thinking. This fourteen-letter word refers to ways of living that can be sustained indefinitely without destroying the natural systems of which we are part. It means saying yes to things like recycling and saying no to things like a second car, which would soon be catastrophic if every family had one.

To attain sustainability we need to **think globally**; we need to understand how the actions of each nation and each person combine to affect the whole world.

To attain sustainability we need to **act locally**; we need to realize that what we do and what our schools do really can make a difference. If we leave the problem to governments nothing will be solved, but if we all do a little in our local area we can control the problem.

To attain sustainability we need to **live as if the future mattered**; we need to live in ways that could be sustained generation after generation if everyone in the world lived that way. This inevitably will involve consuming far fewer resources than we do today in the rich nations.

Schools for a Future

To become a sustainable school requires some environmental planning. First it is necessary to know how your school currently harms or helps the environment – this requires an **environmental audit.**

It is then necessary to get everyone – pupils, staff, governors, parents – to agree to an **environmental policy** in order to implement changes to what everyone involved does and to the way the school is run.

Both an environmental audit and an environmental policy could be produced with the children as part of their existing lessons.

Z1. **Creating a Classroom Environmental Policy**

As everyone in a class will have their own beliefs and values concerning their environment, every classroom policy will be different. It is important that children create their own policy through discussion. This will result in a policy that they 'own' and identify with.

Step 1 is to create a long list of all activities, issues, areas and ideas that could be included in a policy. This is best achieved through **brainstorming**. The ideal group size for this is five to seven and the exercise should take about 12 minutes. Explain the golden rule of brainstorming before you start – every idea, however odd, is to be listed and nothing is to be criticized. Ideas could include 'turning off the lights' and 'not dropping litter in the playground', etc.

Step 2 involves choosing the most important issues. Ask each child to pick two ideas **that are not their own** and say briefly why they feel these are the most important ones. The same ideas can be picked more than once by different children. This may take 10 minutes.

Step 3 is to turn the ideas into policies. Each child can write two one-sentence policy statements on a slip of paper, which can then be glued on to a master sheet.

Z2. Organizing an Environmental Audit

The class environmental audit is based on the policy they have created. Monitoring ensures that the policy is actually used. Once the policy is in use, children can suggest how to check that it is working. For example, two children could have the task of counting, once a week, the number of bits of litter in a section of the playground. Another pair could count, each week, how many lights have been left on in empty classrooms. These results could be displayed as graphs. (See also *Eco School*, by Prue Poulton and Gillian Symons, WWF School Design Project.)

Z3. Creating a Sustainable Garden

Gardens are a widespread ecological symbol in the world's religions, representing both natural and spiritual harmony. Creating a garden is an ideal method for a school to improve its grounds whilst contributing to environmental education and moral and spiritual development. Existing projects in schools include meditation gardens or 'stilling areas', wildlife gardens, Bible gardens (with plants mentioned in the Bible) and nature sanctuaries in neighbouring churchyards. Contact Learning through Landscapes (details overleaf) for ideas.

A new garden could be opened with a celebratory activity (such as the 'Tree of Faiths' activity below) or on a suitable date such as Tu B'Shevat (the Jewish festival of trees) or National Tree Day.

Z4. The Tree of Faiths

The tree is decorated with coloured banners representing the world's religious traditions. Each banner is covered with scriptural quotes on an ecological theme (e.g. trees, creation stories, care for the earth).

Tree Dressing Day is in the first week in December, when trees will not be damaged by decorations. It is organized by Common Ground, P.O. Box 25309, London NW3 1ZA (Tel./Fax 0171 267 2144)

Even as a tree has a single trunk, but many branches and leaves, so there is one true and perfect Religion, but it becomes many religions as it passes through the human medium. The one Religion is beyond all speech; imperfect men put it into such language as they can command, and their words are interpreted by other men equally imperfect. Hence the necessity of tolerance, which does not mean indifference to one's own faith, but a more intelligent and purer love for it. True knowledge of Religion breaks down barriers between faith and faith.

MAHATMA GANDHI (YERAVDA MANDIR, 1945, PAGES 38–40)

● Resources and Addresses

(P) *Indicates a book specifically written for children.*

General

Brown, E. *Harvest Festival in World Religions*. National Society, 1992, ISBN 1 874 340 00 5.

Jeffers, S. *Brother Eagle, Sister Sky*. Hamish Hamilton, 1998, ISBN 0 4054 514 X.

Morgan, P. and Lawton, C. (eds) *Ethical Issues in Six Religious Traditions*. Edinburgh University Press, 1996, ISBN 0 7486 0709 9.

Read, G., Rudge, J., Howarth. R. and Teece, G. *How Do I Teach RE?* The Westhill RE Centre (address on page 110), ISBN 0 7487 1470 7.

Values and Visions – A Handbook for Spiritual Development and Global Awareness. Hodder & Stoughton, 1995, ISBN 0 340 64412 5.

Williams, V. *Green Beliefs: Valued World*. Christian Education Movement (address on page 110).

Stilling, Creative Visualization, Meditation

Day, J. *Creative Visualisation with Children*. Element, 1994, ISBN 1 85230 469 3.

Herzog, Stephanie. *Joy in the Classroom*. The University of Trees Press, California, 1982, ISBN 0 916438 46 5. Developing meditation with children in the primary classroom.

Sherwood, C. *Making Friends with Ourselves*. Kidsmed, 1995, ISBN 0 9525723 0 3. A delightful book which introduces meditation to children.

Stone, M. K. *Don't Just Do Something, Sit There*. Religious and Moral Education Press, ISBN 1 85175 105 X.

Experiencing Nature

Carson, R. *The Sense of Wonder*. Harper & Row, 1965.

Cornell, J. *Sharing Nature with Children*. Dawn Publications, California, available from Deep Books (address on page 110).

Cornell, J. *Sharing the Joy of Nature*. Dawn Publications, California, available from Deep Books (address on page 110).

Cornell, J. *Listening to Nature*. Dawn Publications, California, available from Deep Books (address on page 110).

Cornell, J. *Journey to the Heart of Nature*. Dawn Publications, California, available from Deep Books (address on page 110).

Tschudin, V. *Seeing the Invisible: A Study of Modern Religious Experiences*. Arkana, available fron the Alister Hardy Research Centre (address on page 110).

School Environmental Projects

Poulton, P. and Symons, G. *Eco School* World Wide Fund for Nature School Design Project, ISBN 0 947613 27 7.

Henry Doubleday Research Association
Ryton Organic Gardens
Ryton-on-Dunsmore
Coventry
West Midlands CV8 3LG
Tel. 01203 303517
E-mail: enquiries@hdra.org.uk
Website: www.hdra.org.uk
(for organic seeds)

Common Ground
P.O. Box 25309
London NW5 1ZA
Tel./Fax. 0171 267 2144
(for resources and information about Tree Dressing Day)

Learning through Landscapes
3rd Floor
Southside Offices
The Law Courts
Winchester
Hampshire SO23 9DL
Tel. 01962 846258
Fax. 01962 869099
E-mail: charity@tcp.co.uk
Website: www.ltl.org.uk
(for advice and resources for use of school grounds)

❋ Buddhism

Aggarwal, M. *I am a Buddhist*. Franklin Watts, ISBN 0 7496 1407 2. Looks at Buddhism through the eyes of a child of the faith living in Britain. (P)

Akong Tulku Rinpoche. *Taming the Tiger*. Rider Press, 1994, ISBN 0 7126 6220 0. Tibetan teachings for improving daily life.

Aoyama, S. *Zen Seeds*. Kosei Publications, 1990. A female Soto Zen Priest writes in plain words about the seeds of enlightenment to be found in everyday life.

Barker, C. *Ananda in Sri Lanka*. Hamish Hamilton, 1984, out of print. The life of Ananda, aged 13, who lives in Sri Lanka. (P)

Batchelor, M. and Brown, K. *Buddhism and Ecology*. Cassell, 1992, ISBN 0 304 32375 6. Buddhists from Japan, Thailand, Sri Lanka, Vietnam, Tibet and the West offer their approaches to ecology and tell of practical activities as well as Buddhist teachings and philosophy.

Chödzin, S. and Kohn, A. *Buddhist Tales.* Barefoot Books, 1997, ISBN 1 898000 27 1.

Dilgo Khyentse Rinpoche. *Enlightened Courage.* Editions Padmakara, 1992, ISBN 2 906949 05 1. This teaching condenses the compassionate path to Buddhahood into practical instructions which make use of all the circumstances of daily life.

Erricker, C. J. *Celebrate Buddhist Festivals.* Heinemann, 1985, ISBN 0 431 06948 4.

Gerstein, M. *Mountains of Tibet.* Barefoot Books, 1987, ISBN 1 898000 45 X.1993. A wonderful story and beautifully illustrated. (P)

Hagbrink Bodil. *The Children from Tibet.* Blackie, 1990, ISBN 0 216 93052 9. A delightful story for children about Tibetans living in exile in Nepal. (P)

His Holiness the Dalai Lama and Rowell, G. *My Tibet.* Thames & Hudson, 1992, ISBN 0 500 01500 7. Personal reflections by His Holiness to match the incredibly beautiful photographs of the land he was forced to flee to in 1959.

Jataka Tales Series. Some magnificent story books for children published by Dharma Publishing, available through book shops or from Wisdom Books (address on page 110). (P)

Jacobsen and Kistensen. *A Family in Thailand.* Wayland, out of print. The story of a Thai family. (P)

Khan, N. I. *Twenty Jataka Tales.* East West Publications, ISBN 0 85692 141 6, available through book shops or from Wisdom Books (address on page 110).

Landaw, J. and Brooke, J. *Prince Siddhartha.* Wisdom Books (address on page 110), 1984, ISBN 0 861710 16 9. The life story of the Buddha well written and beautifully illustrated. Suitable for ages 7+ but can be adapted for younger children. (P)

Ringu Tulku Rinpoche. *The Boy Who Had a Dream.* Findhorn Press, 1995, ISBN 1 899171 10 X. A nomadic folk tale from Tibet. (P)

Surya Das. *The Snow Lion's Turquoise Mane.* HarperCollins, 1993, ISBN 0 06 250849 0. Brings together more than 150 authentic tales from Tibet – most of them translated into English for the first time.

Snelling, J. *Buddhism and Buddhist Festivals.* Wayland, out of print. Suitable for children aged 9–11. (P)

Thich Nhat Hanh. *Being Peace.* Parallax Press, 1987, ISBN 0 938077 00 7. Describes the importance of internal peace in order to bring harmony. Parts can be adapted for use by children.

Thich Nhat Hanh. *Call Me By My True Names.* Parallax Press, 1993, ISBN 0 938077 61 9. The collected poems of Thich Nhat Hanh, a Vietnamese monk now living in France. Parts can be adapted for use by children.

Titmuss, C. *The Green Buddha.* Insight Books, 1995, ISBN 1 899289 00 3. Explores the teachings of the Buddha and the relevance of spirituality to national and global issues.

Venerable Sucitto Bhikkhu. *Buddha-Nature.* World Wide Fund for Nature, 1989, out of print. Some reflections on the relationship between Buddhism and the natural world.

Kevin Fossey
The Dharma School
The White House
Ladies Mile Road
Patcham
Brighton BN1 8TB
Tel. 01273 502055
(for information on Buddhist ecological projects)

✝ Christianity

Bellett, E. and Philbrick, M. *For People: For Planet.* Traidcraft Exchange, Kingsway, Gateshead, Tyne & Wear NE11 0NE. Tel. 0191 491 0591. An active learning pack for children aged 7–11.

Breuilly, E. and Palmer, M. *Christianity and Ecology.* Cassell, 1992, ISBN 0 304 32374 8.

Cooper, T. *Green Christianity.* Spire, ISBN 0 340 52339 5. Or call Christian Ecology Link: Tel. 01423 871616.

Farmery, M. *Divine and Human Creativity.* Seeds. Tel. 0181 364 9652. E-mail: seeds30@aol.com.

Green, J. *God's Fool.* Hodder & Stoughton, ISBN 0 340 39077 8. (P)

Handle with Care. CAFOD/Christian Aid, available from Christian Aid (address on page 110). A teacher resource pack exploring a Christian response to development and the environment.

Hastings, S. *Children's Illustrated Bible.* Dorling Kindersley, ISBN 0 7513 5113 X. (P)

Here I Am. CAFOD pack for primary schools. CAFOD (Education), 2 Romero Close, Stockwell Road, London SW9 9TY. Tel. 0171 733 7900. Fax. 0171 274 9630.

Taking Care. Looking at the environment from a Christian perspective. Christian Aid (address on page 110).

ॐ Hinduism

The Higher Taste. Bhaktivedanta Book Trust.

Devi, Y. *The Art of Indian Vegetarian Cooking.* Bala Books.

Both the above are available from BBL, Unit 3, The Terrace, Manor Way, Borehamwood, Herts WD6 1NB. Tel. 0181 905 1244.

Rose, J. *Hindu Story and Symbol.* BFSS National RE Centre (address on page 110).

Friends of Vrindavan
10 Grafton Mews
London W1P 5LF

ISKCON Educational Services
Bhaktivedanta Manor
Hilfield Lane
Aldenham
Herts WD2 8EZ
Tel. 01923 859578
Fax. 01923 852896

Mr K. Patel
Swami Narayan Mandir
105/119 Brentfield Road
Neasden
London NW10 8JP
Tel. 0181 965 2651
(for information about the Mandir and to arrange school visits)

The Young Indian Vegetarians
c/o Nitin Mehta
226 London Road
West Croydon
Surrey CR0 2TF
Tel. 0181 681 8884

☾ Islam

Baring, A. and Blacker, T. *The Birds who Flew beyond Time*. Barefoot Books, ISBN 1 898000 00 X.

O'Brien, J. and Khalid, F. *Islam and Ecology*. Cassell, 1992, ISBN 0 304 32377 2.

Johnson-Davies *The Island of Animals*. Quartet Books, ISBN 0 7043 70166 6. About the status of human beings and their responsibility to the animal kingdom.

Rose, J. *Islamic Story; Folklore and Pattern*. BFSS National RE Centre (address on page 110).

Subhanallah *The Wonders of Creation in the Holy Quran*. World Federation of KSI Muslim Communities, UK, 1993, ISBN 0 95 09879 1 3.

The Islamic Foundation for Ecology and Environmental Sciences
57 Brecon Road
Birmingham B20 3RW
Tel. 0121 523 4264

The Islamic Foundation
Markfield Dawah Centre
Ratby Lane
Markfield Leicester LE67 9RN
Tel. 0530 244944/5
(for slides of Islamic subjects)

The Ismaili Centre
1–7 Cromwell Gardens
South Kensington
London SW7 2SL
Tel. 0171 581 2071
(to arrange school visits to the Islamic garden)

✡ Judaism

Cone, M. *Listen to the Trees*. UAHC Press, 1995, ISBN 0 8074 0536.

Gellman, M. *Does God Have a Big Toe?* HarperCollins, 1989, ISBN 0 06 440453 6. (P)

Let the Earth Teach You Torah. Shomrei Adamah (address below).

Rose, A. *Judaism and Ecology*. Cassell, 1992, ISBN 0 304 32378 0.

The Noah Project
Jewish Education
Celebration and Action for the Earth
P.O. Box 1828
London W10 5RT

Jewish National Fund
58-70 Edgware Way
Edgware
Middlesex HA8 8GQ
Tel. 0181 421 7600
Fax. 0181 905 4299
E-mail: jnf@ort.org

Shomrei Adamah (Keepers of the Earth)
50 West 17th St
New York 10011
Tel. 212 807 6376
Fax. 212 924 5112
E-mail: shomadam@aol.com

Coalition on the Environment and Jewish Life
443 Park Avenue South, 11th Floor
New York 10016-7322
E-mail: coejl@aol.com

Publishers and Resource Centres

BFSS National RE Centre
Brunel University
Osterley Campus
Borough Road
Isleworth
Middlesex TW7 5DU
Tel. 0181 891 8324
Fax. 0181 891 8325

Christian Aid
P.O. Box 100
London SE1 7RT
Tel. 0171 620 4444
E-mail: info@christian-aid.org.uk
Website: www.christian-aid.org.uk

Christian Education Movement
Royal Buildings
Victoria Street
Derby DE1 1GW
Tel. 01332 296655
Fax. 01332 343253
E-mail: cem@cem.org.uk

Deep Books
London SE8 5RT
Tel. 0171 232 2747

Religious Experience Research Centre & Alister Hardy Society
Westminster College
Oxford OX2 9AT
Tel. 01865 247644 ext. 4246

The National Society's RE Centre
36 Causton Street
London SW1P 4AU
Tel. 0171 932 1190/1191

Westhill RE Centre
Westhill College
Selly Oak
Birmingham B29 6LL
Tel. 0121 415 2258
Fax. 0121 415 5399
E-mail: a.leech@westhill.ac.uk

Wisdom Books
402 Hoe Street
London E17 9AA
Tel. 0181 520 5588
E-mail: 100060,2464@compuserve.com
Website: www.demon.co.uk/wisdom

World Wide Fund for Nature
Education Department
Panda House
Weyside Park
Godalming
Surrey GU7 1XR
Tel. 01483 426444
Tel. 01753 643104 for book enquiries
Website: www.wwf-uk.org/education

Index of Activities

Exploring and Reflecting

These activities are designed to help children explore and reflect upon religious teachings about the natural world. The sections at the beginning of each chapter covering the teachings explored and reflected upon in these activities are indicated as follows:

T – Teachings about the World   **M** – Moral Teachings
S – Spiritual Teachings   **V** – Visions of the Future

* These activities could be used (adapted if necessary) in units of work on other faiths.

Exploring and Reflecting

Acting

These activities can follow on from the activities exploring and reflecting on religious beliefs and values.

REEP

The Religious Education and Environment Programme

REEP provides a down-to-earth approach to religious education, moral and spiritual development and assemblies through a range of tailor-made training events for teachers. It is founded on the conviction that concern for nature is essential to religion and that religious awareness has a vital contribution to make to respect for nature.

In addition to training sessions REEP organizes several lectures each year on the spiritual roots of the environmental crisis. Around 50 past lectures, by religious leaders and key environmentalists, are available on cassette. Members receive details about these and a newsletter once a term. Their fee also supports our educational work.

How to take part in our courses

I would like information about REEP's training sessions for teachers.
Please give details about your requirements or tick as appropriate:

| I am a: | ❏ school teacher | ❏ trainee teacher | ❏ headteacher |
| | ❏ advisor | ❏ inspector | ❏ tutor |

| I am mainly concerned with the education of children aged: | ❏ 5–7 | ❏ 7–11 | ❏ 11–14 | ❏ 14–16 |

I am interested in training in:	❏ Religious Education	❏ Environmental Education
	❏ Assemblies	❏ Use of the School Grounds
	❏ Moral and Spiritual Development	
	❏ Other	

| I am interested in: | ❏ full-day events | ❏ half-day events | ❏ 'twilight sessions' |

Further details: ....

I would like to support the work of **REEP**

Please tick as appropriate:
❏ I wish to become a member. Please send a Banker's Order Form.
❏ I wish to become a member and enclose a fee of £11.00 for one calendar year.
❏ I wish to make a donation. Please send a Covenant Form.
❏ I wish to make a donation and enclose £_____
❏ I wish to order_____ copy/ies of this book at £14.95 each and enclose £_____

REEP is a programme of Friends of the Centre. Registered Charity No. 1000998.

School/Institution *(if applicable)* ....

Headteacher *(if applicable)* ....

Name ....

Post *(if applicable)* ....

Address ....

.... Postcode

Telephone .... Fax .... E mail ....

Please Photocopy and complete

Please make cheques payable to **'REEP'**

Please return to **REEP, 8th Floor, Rodwell House, Middlesex Street, London E1 7HJ**

Telephone: 0171 377 0604. Fax: 0171 247 2144.
E mail: reep@globalnet.co.uk Website: www.users.globalnet.co.uk/~reep